THE CLOWNING OF
AMERICA

Woke Capital, Con Inc, and Meme Culture

ORWELL GOODE

THE CLOWNING OF AMERICA

AMERICA

Woke Capital, Con Inc, and Meme Culture

ORWELL GOODE

CONTENTS

INTRODUCTION

*"Do not be so open-minded that your brains
fall out."*
—G.K. Chesterton

*"Democracy is the art and science of running the
circus from the monkey cage."*
—H.L. Mencken

*"The price good men pay for indifference to public
affairs is to be ruled by evil men."*
—Plato

*"Americans may have no identity, but they do have
wonderful teeth."*
—Jean Baudrillard

IDEAS MATTER – and that's about it. Nothing else. Nada. Zilch. It doesn't matter if all the stunning landmarks are obliterated to ash as long as the ideas which set the American Experiment into motion prevail. You could be living in a favelafied mudheap in an equatorial country, but, as long as you defer to The Constitution™ and have an incomplete practical knowledge of Lockean Homesteading, you will be in America. This is what counts, ideas: ideas meant to stand the test of time and mass immigration. It's a cliché to say so, but the placeholder of ideas known as America stands at a crossroads. Well, it would be correct to say that America stood at a crossroads 55 years ago and the choice was already made. Now, it is merely reaping the fruits that it sowed. It has become something of a meme to say something along the lines of "if you were to show a picture of current America to all of those who were willing to make the ultimate sacrifice before heading off to some overseas war, would they still give their life for the future which is now being lived?"

All that matters is atomized individualism and an abstraction of 'free markets'. Conservative values can be distilled into 'limited government'; at a time where the government has grown far beyond our wildest dreams and the newly-arrived underclass of welfare recipients or cheap labor can vote for 'big government' policies, en masse. Family, tradition, and nation are outmoded concepts to be supplanted by something trendier, hipper, browner. Why restrict your ability to consume by troubling yourself with oppressive social constructs? Besides, children are bad for the environment and prevent you from acquiring immediate dopamine surges in the form of consumer goods, experiences, Twitter virtue signals, sex, and/or drugs. Anything and everything your grandparents loved is bad: it was sullied by their internalized racism which manifests itself in systemic and structural white supremacy, thus jading any opinions they may have on cultural affairs since they implicitly wish to preserve their white cultural hegemony – or something. Critical thinking is only acceptable within a narrow hijacked liberal paradigm within the Narrative Complex (Academia, Entertainment, The Mainstream Media). Any other views simply cannot be entertained, since they would reveal themselves as heretical under the progressive moral framework, and, therefore, undeserving of any serious treatment, since they simply can't be true! Any resurrection of old ideas must be discarded as it would interfere with the inevitable march of progress. Where are we progressing to? Who knows?! Who cares. As long as politicians remain in office, collect handsome remuneration, kickbacks, and have their pensions secured – what does it matter? Corporations will continue to rig the market through intensely lobbying morally weak politicians to the detriment of the rest of the nation. As long as they get theirs and the consumer lives in an unstable, materialistic, insane asylum – as long as they keep producing, then consuming, rinse, repeat – what does anything matter anymore?

Over the past few years, memes with a politically-charged message have risen to prominence on social media. Their effectiveness on certain platforms has been startling, even drawing negative coverage from the press. For example, Pepe The Frog, who initially began as a cartoon, was co-opted by the pro-Trump right in the run up to the 2016 US Presidential Election. The cheeky amphibian was often depicted in humorous or weird situations to promote a political case in its imagery. Several publications took to furiously denouncing Pepe: the SPLC and ADL added the quirky frog as a 'hate symbol', Hillary Clinton added an 'explainer' for the whimsical amphibian on her campaign website, and Pepe's creator officially killed him off as a character due to his recoded connotations. Memes seem to carry a significant amount of power crammed into its borders. Memes, to be effective and amusing, need to be rooted in truth or a truth closer to one's lived experiences. The internet is where those alienated by the Narrative Complex's characterizations, plots, deconstruction, and stories seek refuge. The internet is where the NEETs, bros, incels, weebs, MGTOW, PUAs, trads, and members of other social fringes or simply disaffected normies can congregate unhindered by a progressive narrative or regulation (to a certain degree, at least). However, as the internet is the final frontier, relatively untarnished by the progressive brush, ideas contrary to the interests of the establishment can flourish. Groups, corporations, and presidential campaigns backed by literally millions of dollars have to freak out in an attempt to demonize users who cheerfully post the frog with a puerile grin. This is the reaction evoked by a glum green frog on the internet doing comical things. The lengths which well-monied serious people go to in order to rid the internet of memes posted by unemployed 19-year-old adderall-poppers should scare you. They are desperate to preserve their narrative. They simply cannot allow people to lift their heads up from the consumerist feeding trough. Keep stimulating your senses, then get excited for the next stimulation. Rinse. Repeat.

Almost all social, political, and economic incentive structures are geared towards present mindedness, consumerism, and socially-masturbatory selfishness. Discipline is to be shunned. Responsibility is to be shirked. And anybody who dares say otherwise is a horrible racist, bigot, xenophobe, homophobe, etc, etc. But the hollow epithets are merely identifiers for those who are not morally invested in the progressive framework. You must become assimilated to the prevailing Socially-Accepted Politics, distract yourself with hollow thrills, or face social – and now, political and economic – ostracism. By espousing views that were socially acceptable views only 20 years ago, you can lose your ability to provide for your family. A luke-warm remark venting your dislike in the direction in which your country is going can land you in hot water. In other words, you may not like where you're going, but you are to love it, or else! Consumer goods and cheap thrills aren't only a distraction from the bigger picture, while suffusing oneself to the progressive narrative, but they are also a palliative for if it all gets too much. Your children and grandchildren may become a hated minority in the country your ancestors founded, but here you go consumer: have 52 ounces of high fructose corn syrup, a designer T-shirt proudly displaying your unwavering support to that brand, and a smart phone where you can upload your recent purchases to social media.

Picking the worst year in American History is prohibitively tough: which year do you pick – 1913 or 1965? Do we put the cart before the horse or the horse before the cart in identifying what could have led to America's demographic demise? Since the explosion in movements and micro-movements during the Civil Rights Era, nothing other than the 1965 Immigration Act has been so destructive to America's demographic fabric. As a result, neighborhoods have changed, states have become unrecognizable, welfare consumption has exploded, crime has soared, living conditions have declines, and certain states have irreversibly changed their voting patterns, in spite of jovial navel-gazing optimism from several pundits. Don't you know? America is merely an idea. You could import millions of people from entirely different continents, who speak different languages, hold different traditions, customs, values, religions, heritages, and create a coherent nation from them. All you need to do is ensure they defer to The Constitution™, have a penchant for free-market capitalism, love guns, and have children – then they can become as American as apple pie. Nobody can pinpoint when, how, or why they could become American, but what's certain is that if they're left unchecked with no given reason to assimilate, they will become American, you racist xenophobe. But if everyone can be American, then nobody is, right? Right? Anyway, don't concern yourself about the future – how does it affect you now? Think of the GDP – that's increased several times over since 1965. That's all thanks to immigrants and global 'free trade'. Think about how expensive your avocado toast might be. The price could skyrocket by 2-3% without a constant flow of immigrants supposedly destined to work for a job that will be automated in a few years, and we can't have that! What's important is that we open our hearts, and our borders. People are suffering now. So what if you know somebody who died because of the contrived opioid crisis, alcoholism, drug addiction, or suicide – they were probably bigots anyway. They were the past of America. The future's now, old man.

The Gods of the GDP must be appeased in order to secure a steady growth. Rural towns becoming deindustrialized is a mild inconvenience for securing marginally cheaper designer goods and exotic vegetables which only affluent city dwellers can afford. A cost benefit analysis determines that the benefit to unfettered immigration outweighs flyover country's old-fashioned way of life. Think of the bigger picture: would you really want a dip in economic productivity by staunching the flow of immigrants from the south? The GDP will take a hit if you were to do that. Hang on a second – if immigration is an invaluable means by which to grow the economy, then why doesn't anybody seem to care about the economies of countries ostensibly suffering a mass exodus of able workers? Perhaps it's because, and excuse my wrong-think here, the remittances sent back home outweigh the brain drain…

The emphasis on economism underlines an underlying materialism that has permeated and corrupted the political right as a viable alternative, while surrendering itself to a liberal paradigm whose logical conclusion has led to the metastasis of various illiberal policies, all at the same time as forbidding itself from practical cures to its own implosion. The American right has boxed itself into a materialistic worldview, which, for its survival, requires the erosion of tradition, relative communal homogeneity, culture, and history in order to fatten the profit margin of their political donors. Mass immigration depresses wage rates of already-depressed native workers, while companies looking to cut costs have the luxury of outsourcing unskilled labor overseas. Immigrants in America have a higher ability to consume goods while earning American wages and welfare, all of which increases both productivity and revenue, and decreases costs. Kerching! Screw social cost, though – that's unimportant. Unity or social cohesion which took generations to forge simply must fall by the wayside. Things passed down intergenerationally will be deemed wicked by a barrage of trendy verbiage and parlance. The supposed reactive force from the right to 'progress' is veritably toothless, effete, and ineffectual – almost by design. They couldn't get drunk in a brewery, laid in a brothel, or hit water if they fell out of a boat. But, hey, they can console themselves by knowing that they held onto their principles! They kept their morals, which nobody outside their normie-unfriendly social sphere adheres to, even though the land is ablaze. They wilfully played a game in which they didn't know the rules, couldn't make the rules, and the rules were changed whenever their opponents were losing. Don't you know? It's those DemoKKKrats who are the real racists!

Culture seems to be snowballing in one direction: leftward. The possibilities and manmade horrors of the current year are endless. The shift seems to be gathering traction and weight, but flinging chunks of their adherents aside when too much traction and weight has been gained. However, practically every institution unanimously supports a leftist cultural worldview. HR and Marketing departments are overtly blazing a cultural trail with their enthusiastic support for social justice. The Narrative Complex has been more subtle with their dissemination of crafty narratives and metanarratives to seep into the public's consciousness over generations. A non-genetic transfer of widespread information is usually known as a meme. And, By Jove! The cultural left are really damn good at it. The difference is that they've sculpted an epistemological framework to cater for an erroneous worldview that doesn't harmonize with human nature when put into practice. This is why 'The Narrative' must be protected at all costs to preserve their cultural hegemony and institutional power. Counternarratives or certain statistics must be suppressed and the exponents of these views silenced. There is too much at stake.

The recent phenomenon of 'drag kids' has arisen at a time where the media's attempt to normalize pedophilia failed. Adverts everywhere promote alternative family arrangements as an affront to so-called "heteronormativity". Political arguments from both sides of the aisle have seemingly failed. As we embark upon an era of 'post-truth' within a heavily democratized environment, not only does democracy become a demographic headcount – at a time when the native population is on the decline – but voters are a slave to their passions, guided by emotions programmed to feel a certain way when facing news or information to reconcile with a progressive moral framework. This mentality was reflected in the 'NPC' meme: a grey-faced anthropomorphized automaton with no free will, but only the ability to parrot cliches, slogans, and to feel a certain preconditioned way to contradictory viewpoints. You can tell just how effective it was in attacking those it meant to represent, as social media would censor those who used the meme as an avatar. In other words, it struck a nerve.

Corporations and state governments seem to be imbued in the same progressive doctrines. What's almost certain is that avoiding the narrative is almost impossible and the cultural shift to the left is inexorable. Conservatives haven't conserved much at all if the media is in the process of normalizing 'drag kids.' Bizarrely, conservatives still offer support for deregulation and tax cuts, much of which benefits large corporations who make a mockery out of all of their values and uniformly support the political aisle which seeks to turn them into a humiliated, demoralized, minority in their own country. Moreover, corporations have worked to silence dissident voices, censor and deplatform, ruin the lives of those outside of the progressive bubble, and encroach upon First Amendment rights. It's a shame we can't stop them; since they're a private company, they can do what they want!

US foreign policy has seen trillions of dollar wasted and innumerable lives lost, while destabilizing portions of the Middle East and Maghreb leading to a Migrant Crisis that rocked Europe a few years ago. The weakening vice grip in their role of global policeman has seen pointless entanglements, regime change, The Patriot Act, and a marked fall in patriotism – admittedly, partly due to mass immigration. How does America benefit from any of this?

Society is becoming increasingly materialistic, alienated, and atomized. Many complaints from the older generations often boil down to a loss of a sense of community. If I cared to venture a blunt diagnosis to the problem – mass immigration – most people in polite society would call me racist, reciting empty platitudes firmly stating, that, in actual fact, diversity is, indeed, our greatest strength. But what if it isn't? What if the colorfully advertised consumer goods serving as a distraction were actually bad? What then? What if the narratives meticulously spun by The Narrative Complex were both inauthentic and demoralizing? Consumerism acts as a means to plaster over the crippling emptiness of modern life while both weakening the resolve of the public and distracting one from the bigger picture. Taking the path of least resistance is most appealing when there is no reason to assume hardship, responsibility, or unnecessary burdens such as the truth itself. The truth is a painful state of consciousness, as it obliterates the conniving narratives representing the world as a peaceful place if it wasn't for those pesky Westerners. We could all sit around a campfire, locking hands, while ingesting natural psychoactives if it weren't for those darned colonizers. The world was a happy place before Columbus set sail. Sure, they may not have had all the post-colonial luxuries they inherited, but still! All that's important is that white history is bad; therefore, resources, land, political power, sovereignty, tax revenue must all be forked over, for the greater good. In the meantime, there's food enriched with high fructose corn syrup and opioids you can indulge on until you perish.

Don't you know? America will be a far better place when you've gone – the press says you can be diversified and replaced, but it's simultaneously a far-right conspiracy theory. Anyway, diversity is a strength, but mass immigration is vengeance for colonialism. In all seriousness, if say, somebody with high neuroticism and low conscientiousness were to write a scathing piece demanding the multiculturalization of Ghana, their good faith and character would be called into question for penning such bileful drivel. However, the narratives have conditioned public consciousness to the point where blatant hatred towards the founding stock is pedestrian.

The Clowning of America didn't happen overnight. At first, there was a hijacking of the Federal Government by financial and corporate interests, requiring large-scale events and catastrophes to consolidate its position of power. Then, new boogeymen had to be created in order to give its heroic causes and consequential aggrandizement legitimacy. The fabric of society had to be both resewn by adding foreign elements into the mix, while weakening the original threads to accommodate the new fabric. Recently, the spiritual and moral gangrene has exposed the skeleton of the rest of the body as brittle. However, the thought of amputation or extirpation of the gangrene is viewed as mean. How will the necrotizing bacteria survive if we amputate the limb? It simply must be tolerated. In fact, tolerating the gangrene isn't enough! The gangrenous limb must become an enduring source of virtue, the pinnacle of moral good, an irreplaceable symbol of exceptionalism. Those who foresaw the cultural, spiritual, and moral decline being the peak of a slippery slope descending into an unscalable pit of decadence are the ones to blame. We have already hit terminal velocity and cut ourselves free from the restrictive parachute of more traditional vistas, so let's see where this goes. It can only go well.

The Clowning of America isn't a tragedy, but a comedy. When I was young, I'd often wonder how great civilizations like Rome could be so dumb as to let themselves wither into dust. But now we can see that there are so many incentive structures that make it extremely difficult to make it worth preserving something greater than oneself. Excess wealth and luxury weakens the population to the point where their prolonged comfort becomes the highest value, rather than swimming against the current in rejecting harmful social trends. While birth rates have plummeted, divorce rates have skyrocketed, implicitly raising social time preferences, and a desire to present mindedly produce and consume towards more immediate gratification. People don't seem to have much skin in the game. The subtext within many prevailing social narratives is to accumulate as many fleeting dopamine hits as possible, while disregarding the naysayers who are moral outsiders to the progressive framework. Don't try to do anything about the slavery to your passions or attempt to unshackle others from theirs. Who are you to judge them? You haven't walked a mile in their shoes! Being guided by passion and the path of least resistance leads to a breakdown of traditional societal norms and paves the way to man made horrors beyond your comprehension. Who would ever thought we'd live to see reputable newspapers promote pedophila, drag kids, and vicious anti-white hatred? A putrid tolerance of demonic narratives will eventually see gradual normalization. A society that tolerates profound racial hatred and pedophilia isn't one worth preserving. The Overton Window, although temporarily halted by populist movements, will continue to shift left, and there are no breaks and no fixed destination. This freight train will keep on rolling until it has been derailed. Life is destined to be a sequence of external stimuli temporarily staving off boredom between production and consumption. Self-serving politicians and upper management of large corporations will be okay though. All statues must fall – not just the problematic ones. Ulysses S. Grant, Abe Lincoln, Teddy Roosevelt, none are sanctified enough to be spared by the mob. If you don't enthusiastically support the erasure of your past, you're the one in the wrong. History dictates identity. History has to be revised, removed, retaught to instill guilt and self-hatred. Identities are to be demolished and then rebuilt around consumerism, under various brand names. The goal is to reduce yourself into a non-resistant, faceless economic unit content with the fruits of the gods of progress.

If you were to tell somebody from fifty years about what's happening now, they wouldn't believe you. They'd think they were conquered by a hostile entity. They'd laugh in your face. But a weary middle America was spiritually conquered by the gods of materialism. The Civil Rights era proved to be the greatest almost-bloodless revolution in history, inverting absolutely everything from family life, so-called "gender roles," power structures, immigration, and so forth, with the end of radically transforming America and the West as a whole. It's gotten to the point where a phrase as innocuous as "all lives matter" becomes grounds for termination of contract and ostracism from polite progressive society. Heaven help you if you say "It's Okay to Be White" or "White Lives Matter" – you'd be literally worse than an Austrian artist-turned-politician. Now, Americans are treated to corporate-sponsored cyclical revolutions. Like clockwork, these revolutions come and go on a yearly basis, only to be discarded for the next thrill. Sadly, the bulk of regular folk – or "normies" – fall for the con. June is Pride Month, which signifies Rainbow filters, flags, emblems, logos, to be proudly beamed across every corporation's banner for the entire month. When July comes around, the Rainbow is quickly dropped. February is Black History Month, which means an extra dose of white guilt to be mustered by the Narrative Complex. Don't forget International Women's Day, or Labor Day, or any other day that has to be enthusiastically supported by everyone. Those remaining silent on these issues are problematic. It means they haven't thrown their support behind the movement of the day. And if there isn't the movement of the day, the mainstream media will concoct some psy-op transgressing their unalienable progressive egalitarian morality. Once that loses traction, the next outrage meant to tug on the heart-strings of the emotionally underdeveloped will be inorganically promoted by the press. And this will be rinsed and repeated ad infinitum.

The 'Clownworld' meme has been particularly effective in mocking the current state of affairs, which have arguably been the real-world application of New Left principles met by a pathetic posturing mainstream right. Reality has drifted so far from an envisaged natural order of things that it can be symbolized by clown-attired frogs. For a position to be refuted, it must at least acknowledge truth, but truth itself is unimportant as draconian measures have been introduced in certain instances for those who do not wholly accept some of the tenets of the prevailing socially-accepted political dogmas. You can't help but laugh. Some of the things we're treated to everyday are pitiful. Life has become so empty that passivity isn't worth disturbing when faced with existential threats. A comatose society is one that is too afraid to address its rapidly changing demographics, sexualization of children, falling birth rates, family breakdown, illegal immigration, welfare participation, criminality, addiction, meaninglessness, contrived guilt, and social atomization. Moreover, since the intelligentsia wholeheartedly support many of the metapolitical changes and lifestyles leading to the aforementioned social ailments, one feels a sense of intellectual reward by espousing these positions flaring up the symptoms of the ailment. It comes to a point where all semblance of morality has been suppressed, then inverted to cater for limitless social freedom. Of course, the economic and social cost of unlimited freedom has been socialized onto others. Tradition must be kept at bay, reviled, then constantly blitzed to render it a worthless alternative. A lifeboat in a tempestuous sea of subjectivity has been shattered in order to spare the rocky sea's temperament. Chaos must reign victorious by demolishing order. Herein enters our antihero…

The clown symbolizes chaos. It embodies a completely dysfunctional person: big feet, unnatural hair, red round nose, white makeup, colorful baggy clothes, squirting flower, unending handkerchief, tiny car, and so on. The purpose of the unorthodoxy of the clown is to evoke laughter from its chaos. Acting foolishly, mockingly, and amiably, the clown captures chaos to the point where wider audiences – particularly children – can not only appreciate and identify order, but that, to a certain extent, understand that what dwells outside order is worthy of derision. This is why clowns spring to mind. Even those who believe themselves to pertain to the prevailing socially-accepted politics can understand the lunacy in certain positions or social events which may have previously been considered absurd. Presently, America seems to be in a free-for-all freefall. The only allowable order is for the abolition of any impediments to chaos. As a country, it appears to have suffered many blows for the immediate personal gain of corrupt individuals. People who have presented themselves as saviors have been either false prophets or ostracized for their vainglory. Politics runs a tiring course. Much of the statesmanship is a distraction to the bigger picture. As H.L. Mencken said, "Democracy is the art and science of running the circus from the monkey cage". He was eerily right.

Trump's 2016 victory only girded the socio-political left. It was a gift to invigorate a perpetually youthful and energetic left-wing political force – one that feels wronged by past events and oppression. Not only is overt power back on the menu, but with talk of reparations and redressing a historical balance, so is revenge. Mainstream conservatism is terminally low-energy. It is something of a cliche to wanna be "hip," "with it," and "hanging with the kids." mainstream conservatism is remarkably out of touch with the culturally ascendant young and diverse left. While there's significant overlap between some policies, both social and economic, a curtailment of immigration, for example, would not prove popular given, perhaps, tribal reasons behind a more diverse youth to be against the restriction of immigration. The media's over-exaggerated portrayal of Trump has prompted histrionics from people who communicate far too much with emojis, claiming that 45 is "literally killing us." The reality is, Trump appears to be another run-of-the-mill conservative president, but his legacy and depiction is akin to something out of the 1920s-30s, which has led to a hyper-energized left but meek results overall.

The purpose of this book is to elucidate a philosophical departure from instinct, demonstrating how a leftist version of classical liberalism has perverted meaning itself to redefine values necessary to preserve a nation as pitiful, evil, malevolent, antiquated, primordial. Instinct has been relegated to the cesspit of history as an atavism reminding rational man of his primordial imperfections. Many of the counternarratives, countermemes, and populist movements, to the liberal, would appear to be thoroughly irrational. However, much of the dissatisfaction exhibited by many seems to be irrational. If economic conditions and material wealth have never been better, then how come average Joes are rejecting the visions of the anointed elites? This book serves to illustrate how narratives mold public consciousness to cement power, as well as exposing a metaphysical chasm between liberalism and the transcendental. This book will also explore metapolitical perspectives on sensitive topics ranging from anti-natalism to theories of time in the usage of one's life on this mortal plane. Amid these serious themes, this book also seeks to humor the reader by adding lashings of dry comedy, because even within the darkest days, there's always something to laugh about.

CHAPTER
1

SEND IN THE CLOWNS

"A time is coming when men will go mad, and when they see someone who is not mad, they will attack him, saying, 'You are mad; you are not like us."

—St. Anthony The Great

AMERICA IS ONE of the most beautiful countries I have ever had the privilege to visit. She is blessed with unrivalled natural beauty, deserts, mountain ranges, diverse climates, lakes, rivers, dramatic scenery, and stunning wildlife. In many parts, Americans are warm, welcoming, and friendly. America has it all. But what it lacks is a political class and a Narrative Complex which loves it as much as its founding stock. Traitorous politicians, profit-seeking corporations, Anti-American special interest groups, and the self-serving Narrative Complex have banded together to alter public consciousness into accepting anti-Americanism in order to delegitimize America as a nation. America is associated with colonialism, genocide, and slavery – definitely something that isn't worth preserving. The European demographic must become displaced, disenfranchised, and diluted by sustained mass immigration. If they protest, call just them "racist", as it will silence them. If they don't like where their country is going, they're bigots – this is progress, this is desirable. The European demographic is what prevents our intellectual and moral superiors from ushering in an age of diverse utopian prosperity. You know, if they just disappeared, we could actually get somewhere. Right? But, in the meantime, through intense propaganda dispersed by the Narrative Complex, America has to become Clownified. Why? Because much of what is packaged as progress is a form of humiliation. And within every power dynamic, those without social power must have their values utterly undermined and grotesquely ridiculed.

America isn't a serious country. America looks to become the embodiment of every claim its enemies make against her. Apart from endless overseas wars, in becoming the global policeman – in fact, worsening the sociopolitical landscape of almost every country it touches – America has allowed itself to fester from within. America has become humiliated by an elite class of individuals who are only beholden to their limitless self-interest. Any enthusiastic resistance to the prevailing socially-accepted politics is put down quicker than a rabid pitbull. Even tepid criticism of progressive narrative is cast asunder. Drawing comparisons to recent, artificially promoted, social change glorifying movements such as 'drag kids' which sexualizes children – given how they're dressed, perform at gay bars, and lusted after by outspoken pedophiles – to clowns as a means to humiliate the extreme progressive worldview. Under almost any other non-western civilization, the 'drag kid' phenomenon would not be tolerated. Sexualizing children would not be tolerated. But, with the sexualization of children comes a further desacralization of sex which tacitly undermines the sanctity of marriage – the nuclear family being foundational to any functioning civilization as a going concern. Humiliation intertwines itself harmonious with materialism. A humiliated society which becomes conscious of its political disenfranchisement is likelier to exhibit ressentiment; this would deglamorize political action as a dignified response, and, it would also relegate the individual to self-debasing palliatives in the form of consumer goods or fleeting experiences.

As an extension to America's problematic past comes a dampening of the patriotic flame. Neoconservatives have backed several foreign unwinnable wars, hijacking, then delegitimizing American patriotism as a standard bearer into these self-destructive entanglements. Patriotism has been repackaged and recoded to signify wanton xenophobia, and not a love for one's country. Patriotism is also indissolubly linked to the much-hated Patriot Act, indelibly linked to scandalous mass surveillance and pointless overseas bloodshed. America's past and present are off-limits for those who dare self-identify as patriots. There must be no core binding principles uniting America as a nation: what only matters is a dehomogenized, cultureless, atomized, and hyper individualistic consumerism. A lot of modern architecture, for example, is bland and boring in order for it to be palatable to the highest number of diverse groups; a pronounced, cultured, unique architecture could come across as daunting and unwelcoming. Like art, architecture represents a spiritual zeitgeist; unfortunately, our current time is inauthentic, confused, spiritually comatose in favor of consumerism – and architecture, more often than not, reflects a spiritual and cultural deprivation.

Tolerance is little more than trendized indifference. There is no love in being tolerant. Tolerance indicates a lack of care. If something were normal, beneficial, or good it would not have to be tolerated. The demand for tolerance is a sugar coated demand for unpleasant concessions, dressed in effete verbiage. Somebody who treats their body with self-respect doesn't just shovel anything into their body – they are intolerant of things which may do them ill, in the future. However, tolerance has been paraded as one of the highest virtues, but, the only thing tolerance instills is inaction and political correctness. For evil to take root within society, society must be tolerant. A vigilant society isn't tolerant. Like an immune system, it combats pathogens from within. Tolerance is an autoimmune disease which attacks white blood cells and prevents the body from healing itself. Without tolerance, Americans wouldn't see the European stock be on course to become a projected minority in the not-so-distant future. Without tolerance, drag kids wouldn't be in the process of being normalized, mainstreamed, by the media. Without tolerance, giving powerful hormones to prepubescent children on a growing scale wouldn't be permitted. Parents responsible for what, in previous times, would be considered abuse, would be prosecuted and shunned for their mistreatment. Tolerance is what allows society to rot from within, leaving little of value worth rescuing. Now, does it really make a difference if millions of third world migrants exploit the immigration process via chain migration, then consume disproportionate levels of welfare per capita? Tolerance has rendered America into nothing more than an idea – a crystallization of self-abolishing liberalism in the ether of human thought. Tolerance has debased America to a multicultural economic region where economic productivity and consumerism is worshipped. But think of the GDP! Think of the DOW! Think of the food! Think of the enrichment! With the exception of the last exclamation, the memeworthy satirization of pro-globalist, pro-immigration, arguments are purely materialistic. The final exclamation attacks a certain cultural staleness towards the winter of civilization – the raison d'etre, the mission, Manifest Destiny has lost its life spark. There is no longer an upward-striving energy to be mustered and an apparent will-to-death or being-towards-death which follows civilization's zenith, consuming cultural thought. After achieving greatness, one becomes self-critical – manifested in the Narrative Complex's anti-Americanism. Moreover, many of those who are self-critical merely received the gift of civilization without dirtying their hands. Exertion was never known. Hardship is beyond living memory. Valuing something one never worked for, but received, is bound to see that something taken for granted.

Tolerance didn't go from 0-60 overnight. No. Tolerance takes time to build. Heroin addicts can take hefty doses which can kill first-time users. Like any addiction, tolerance is built by experience. In the case of the dramatic social change in America away from exceptionalism, tolerance had to be increased gradually. Like a slowly boiled frog – whose metabolism cannot perceive the rising temperature of the water – the Narrative Complex has skilfully adopted a gradualist approach in desensitizing public consciousness into accepting social mores deemed unacceptable in a not-so-distant past. The idea of drag kids, graphically sexual TV shows, and radical demographic changes all required a certain incrementalism in order to become accepted. If there were to be a sudden change from an idyllic 1950s America to 2019 America, there would be a revolt. Today's hyper-tolerance was brought to life through a slow metamorphosis becoming part of a moral framework: you cannot criticize tolerance, only pre-existing social constructs which impeded social liberalism. Traditional forms of morality and governance are, by default, automatically outmoded. Anything dwelling outside of the progressive orbit cannot be tolerated. Tolerance is a form of social currency. One can score social brownie points by virtue signaling to their peers their higher state of tolerance to social taboos. By liberating those oppressed by traditional morality and Western social constructs, one can feel a sense of grandeur by uplifting the few at the expense of the many. The overuse of tolerance as a virtue has become a vice – on social media, virtue signaling for a spike in engagement can be related to a well-deserved dopamine hit. Tolerance the modern ideal. Tolerance, through intense Narrative Complex propaganda, has been instinctively linked to goodness. Bad people don't tolerate intolerance. Instead, they must practice understanding for what they can't quite comprehend. Social pressures and incentive structures within the liberal/progressive paradigm reward tolerance. In the past, intolerance was necessary to ensure social, moral, and demographic stability. Intolerance is one of the most masculine virtues. Today, however, masculinity is being defecated on from a great height by the Narrative Complex – in particular, feminist academics, bloggers, and journalists – as metapolitically undesirable traits such as masculinity must be suppressed in order to secure the progressive cultural hegemony. A masculine society would never tolerate the current horrors beyond prior comprehension. Men need to be metaphorically castrated in order to bring about a more egalitarian, anti-nationalist, anti-hierarchical, society. In some cases, they are even being doped up on female hormones to control their masculine behavior. Men tend to be more seditious than women, on the whole, when faced with tyranny. By destroying masculinity, then rendering the remnants of masculinity 'uncool', society becomes more tolerant, and thus, easier to manipulate for sociopolitical and economic ends.

The destruction of the nuclear family, closely followed by the rise in single motherhood, has given rise to an emasculated country with little notable leadership at an individual level. In tearing families apart – through a combination of ideological propaganda, consumerism, and the Narrative Complex – children have been left without suitable role models and parental balance. Boys raised in a broken home, more often than not, will be lacking any adequate force to channel their masculinity. Boys are constantly told by the Narrative Complex – feminist teachers at school, pernicious media/entertainment on TV – that their masculinity is inherently evil. And because of the sustained anti-male – and anti-white – propaganda, a lot of boys are being considered defective within gynocentric spaces such as public education and the Entertainment Industry. Quite simply, a masculine de-androgenized society wouldn't put up with consistent anti-American propaganda. Those most involved in progressive culture tend not to have high testosterone. Studies confirm that men with relatively lower levels of testosterone tend to be on the political left. This is because men with lower levels of testosterone won't be as naturally competitive, directly aggressive, confident, assertive, etc. A quick un-nuanced distillation of leftism would be to generalize leftist positions as favoring 'big government' with a generous redistributive economy. Instead of competing for resources, a more powerful entity extracts resources and redistributes them to more economically vulnerable members of society. Masculinity is also conflated with hierarchy, order, stability, reciprocity, merit-based respect, and discipline; the progressive order cannot tolerate or survive these masculine traits. Hierarchy is intrinsically anti-egalitarian as it recognizes problematic essentialism and differing human abilities. In the same way, order stands contrary to modern progress, as it would render its existence not only redundant but also socially harmful. Stability, like order, is anti-progress: progress cavalierly charges into socially uncharted territory; stability requires truth, morality, and customs to be embedded in something, rather than being rootless. Reciprocity is impossible in a society where social and economic parasitism is destigmatized and naysayers are vilified. Merit-based respect has become undermined by programs designed to create egalitarian outcomes; in affirmative action programs, the best person isn't chosen for the degree or job – whoever has been most oppressed wins out. Discipline, in a traditional sense, is further anathema to progress. Discipline requires a repudiation of temptation, goal orientation, repetition, and a perception of unchangeability: if goals, information, knowledge, values, language, etc, constantly changed, then, the initial reason to be disciplined would become pointless and invalidated.

CHAPTER
2

LIBERALISM

*"I must add… my gratitude to you for the attention
with which you have listened to me, for, from my
numerous observations, our Liberals are never
capable of letting anyone else have a conviction of
his own without at once meeting their opponent
with abuse or even something worse."*
—Fyodor Dostoevsky, *'The Idiot'*

AMERICA WAS FOUNDED on liberalism. Today, contemporary interpretations of liberalism have rendered public figures to make reductive pronouncements asserting that America is basically an idea and not a country. The fabric of America is also attacked within the phrase "a nation of immigrants," which was coined before the 1965 Immigration Act, which added another perverse layer to mix. Some have described modern (urban) America as one giant strip mall. Nature, countryside, and wildlife are disregarded in favor of consumerism. But this is in keeping with America's liberal ontology.

Liberalism itself can be pretty broad to describe as it encompasses the bulk of modern political ideologies. In fact, very few current political ideologies are free from the influence of liberalism. Ideologies ranging from anarcho-capitalism – classical liberalism taken to its radical logical conclusion – to social democracy, find their roots in liberalism. Socialism itself, although somewhat predating liberalism as a concept, in its current radical form was born out of a dialectical reaction of classical liberalism, in particular, British industrialism. For the purpose of this book, the main facets of liberalism, which can be used in some ways interchangeably with liberalism include capitalism, rationalism (including some forms of empiricism), materialism, forming the same political Leviathan, although nothing like the one that Hobbes describes.

Both the mainstream left and right embrace forms of liberalism. The left takes an acquiescent stance to neoliberal economics, while at the same time championing general welfare, regulation, and steeper tax rates. The trade-off is acceptance of modern progressive social policies. If anything, neoliberal economics serves as an engine room to promote, intensify, and further progressive social policies. The right promotes increased market deregulation, lower tax rates, and fewer public services. The right pays lip service to traditionalist values, but simultaneously panders to leftist social positions such as pro-LGBT, pro-immigration, and feminism, thus undermining their supposed 'conservative' values. The two factions represented by the Democrats and Republicans offer very little in terms of policy. A feature, not a bug, of two-party politics is that radical change would rock the political order and prove undesirable for the powers-that-be. There needs to be sufficient stability to project the illusion of democratic choice. This is why there appears to be a synthesis of right and left wing liberalism, characterized by their economic stances. The left is the socially proactive force of modern society. Most, if not all, of the recent societal shifts are dictated by their think tanks and activists. Of course, this comes with great assistance from the Narrative Complex. In a liberal society, morals or values aren't backed by a social belief in anything eternal and are, therefore, subject to constant change. Having identified the left as a proactive force of social change, the right is a poorly synthesizing reactive force. The right, in a liberal society, acts as a speedbump, but also a rearguard defense circling the wagons around social change to represent that change's normalization. At the time of writing this book, one social change which is in the process of becoming fully normalized is 'drag queens.' Not all mainstream conservatives have embraced the change with open arms, but groups such as Turning Point USA have begun to use a 'drag queen' activist to churn out rehashed liberalized talking points, on the one hand, recoding conservatism to signify homosexual corporate libertarianism, and, on the other, normalizing drag queens to out-left the left.

When people say that the left-right dichotomy is outdated, they aren't fully wrong. Without liberalism, there wouldn't be much of a need for the left-right dichotomy, which would be used to describe one's economic preference; more government interference on the left, less government interference on the right. Liberalism itself has been split between classical liberalism and neoliberalism to refer to a shift in its meaning. In my chapter on Metapolitics, I go on to identify the main points of departure between the traditional left and right. Here, liberalism should be identified as a form of materialism. A new dichotomy separating materialism from the transcendental should be implemented as the lines are less blurred than of the liberal left-right paradigm.

CHAPTER
3

MEMES

"They are ACTUALLY using illegal memes!"
—Thomas Wictor

"Like computer viruses, successful mind viruses will tend to be hard for their victims to detect. If you are the victim of one, the chances are that you won't know it, and may even vigorously deny it."
—Richard Dawkins

DEFINITION OF MEME according to Dictionary.com

noun

- a cultural item that is transmitted by repetition and replication in a manner analogous to the biological transmission of genes.
- a cultural item in the form of an image, video, phrase, etc., that is spread via the Internet and often altered in a creative or humorous way.

Memes are fun. They really are. Like meth, they're often cooked up in sunless basements. Memes are problematic. Memes, to be funny, must be brief, pithy, and grounded in truth. They came under close scrutiny during and after the 2016 US presidential election for the supposed message of hate they delivered. Hate, in this context, is employed as an identifier of something politically incorrect – a counternarrative to the progressive narrative. Anything disliked by the adherents of the prevailing socially-accepted politics is deemed 'hateful'. Whether or not hate is a driver of the message behind the meme is irrelevant; what's important is that the message reveals itself as an existential threat to the integrity of a certain narrative. While certain memes can come across as lewd or gory, the metanarrative within the meme is what matters – and what must be combated by those who wish to preserve a pre-existing narrative. The internet is where people who have fled the prevailing Pop Culture and its politically-laden narratives to seek safe refuge from a foisted worldview which doesn't match up to their lived experiences. On the internet is where these people looking to escape can congregate, communicate, exchange ideas, and avoid metapolitical messaging urging them to live inauthentically. Here is where memes carrying alternative viewpoints can go viral, being passed on by hundreds or thousands of users. These memes resonated with people on message boards or social media who seek to avoid being alienated by the not-so-subtle propagandizing by the Narrative Complex. Those who espoused many of the views held within the counternarratives would be considered on the political right. The current narratives overwhelmingly side with the political left: in culture, entertainment, lifestyle, etc.

"The Left can't meme" is a common phrase that is often thrown around by those on the political right, especially when they come face to face with another wall of text posted by some blue-haired activist on Twitter. The truth is, they can and can't. The left CAN absolutely meme – and their memes are one hell of a lot more successful than right-wing memes, plus they're backed by billions – if not trillions – of dollars. Their memes are movies, comedy, entertainment, magazines, commercials at sporting events, woke capital, and education. The left's memes are firmly integrated and have become unshakable parts of everyday existence. However, the left, on the whole, cannot meme on the internet. Many of the 'left's' mainstream political sympathies find themselves aligned within the Narrative Complex's paradigm. This means that their lives experiences and understanding of things coincide more with the non-internet political memes such as Entertainment or Woke Capital. Therefore, among internet users who have conditioned themselves to be less receptive to the messaging from the Narrative Complex can sift out memes that 'miss' the point. Part of the nature of internet memes is to be dissident, revolutionary, edgy – repackaged walls of text repeating much of the political establishment's positions simply do not resonate with those who reject Pop Culture. Moreover, there's a certain excessive roundaboutness to left-wing memes in an attempt to debunk right-wing positions or to put forth left-wing ones, leaving the beholder of the meme overwhelmed. Memes, to be effective, must be rooted in truth and brevity.

A Brief Note on Boomer memes

BOOMER MEMES ARE SIMPLY AWFUL, TOO. The reason is similar to that of why left-wing memes are ineffective on the internet. The lived experience of boomer conservatism dwells within the narrative as part as a mitigated reaction to inevitable blowback from certain policies. However, it isn't a rejection of the Narrative Complex, but a willingness to play along – and to try to beat them at their own game, which, sadly, has been an exercise in futility. The cringeworthiness of boomer memes arises from an utter disconnection in spheres of reality between their generation and the younger factions of the internet right. Many of the grifters and gatekeepers hoisted up to be revered right-wing figures keep boomer conservatives pinned into a narrative which poses no threat to private interests. Their tone, demeanor, language, desires, and ends, infrequently coincides with anybody who 'memes' politically on the internet. Additionally, their poor photoshopping skills and clumsy wording rubs salt into the wound.

Effective memes require a short message. Walls of text lose humor, making eyes roll. Memes are best for evoking emotions, usually humor. Given how we are moving into an era of 'post-truth', feelings – not facts – are what guides us in our political decision making. If somebody has been raised in an environment where they face nothing more than prevailing socially-accepted politics, their feelings will be attuned accordingly. With much of the narratives we're transmitted, a certain moral waywardness is associated with those whose views linger outside of orbit of the prevailing socially-accepted politics. Anybody can be pre-programmed into feeling a certain way when facing differing viewpoints. Jonathan Haidt found that liberals and conservatives activated different parts of their brains when attempting to handle identical tasks. Shielding individuals from differing views can pose itself as a disservice to the formation of an individual in the name of nurture or protecting their feelings. And, unfortunately, in addition to post-truth, it seems that people's feelings don't care about facts. Memes aren't lengthy hyper-rationalist treatises trying to convince people of a nuanced esoteric position, but simply there to evoke an emotional response mostly in the form of humor. Other emotions from memes can include anger, disgust, and guilt.

Guilt is a powerful emotional tool: it can lead to a quasi-suicidal sense of indebtedness in the form of self-destructive policies and cultural decay. In the sense of the Western World, millions have been guilted into hating oneself. On the one hand, Westerners must feel a collective sense of guilt in all the revised atrocities committed by a select few individuals. On the other hand, they cannot feel triumph in the marvellous accomplishments of others. They can only swallow the bitter pill: their forebears are responsible for hideous evils by today's effete and morally fraudulent standards, while assuming that all their accomplishments are merely products of oppression – which the supposedly oppressed groups are suffering today. To rectify the situation, guilt must be an omnipresent emotion to declaw Americans, in this instance, from resisting undesirable policies and radical social change. Guilt ushers in a crushing sense of nihilism, worthlessness, and self-loathing – self-loathing for actions which the individual alone isn't responsible. It seems that guilt spiritually oppresses people to the point where they wish for their own demise or the end of their genetic lineage for the actions of their ancestors seen through a revisionist lens.

Emotion vs Counteremotion

EMOTIONS ARE POWERFUL TOOLS – especially in our post-truth world. Emotions, instead of reason, guide people into forming their opinions. Most are exclusively exposed to one side's talking points without an ideological counterbalance. As I explained earlier regarding the NPC meme, people have become finely tuned feelers, not thinkers. Think, if you will, what it must be like to be exposed to one set of viewpoints, to have any outsider views demonized as blasphemous or heretical, to have the character of the exponents of those roguish views besmirched, to go through one's formative years, education, social life, and so on, strongly believing in these views throughout one's life. Your parents, teachers, TV, peers all told you it wasn't just good or morally right, but it also felt good to be associated with this identity too. You got a kick, a dopamine hit off what you believed in addition to a sense of belonging. Give me the boy and I'll give you the man. Politics, in a democratic circus, is a relentless evocation of emotion: children suffering at the border, refugee children going hungry, children dying from relentless gun violence. I think you all know which demographics would be more responsive to these pleas.

There are two predominant emotions with balancing counteremotions which are manifest:

- Guilt vs Anger/Wrongdoing
- Tolerance vs Disgust

Guilt is a particularly pernicious tool to not only politically disarm people – be they worthy of said guilt or not – but also to shepherd guilty individuals into promoting political causes at odds with their best interests. For example, white guilt has been one of the most salient forms of guilt looming over the political circus. It's fair to say it is an extremely pernicious form of guilt, in that it potentially ruins tens of thousands of lies thanks to incessant propaganda, narratives, and social pressures into accepting guilt for acts somebody didn't commit. An unrevised version of those blighted by white guilt has been withheld from these individuals, while exaggerating the worst elements of white history to instill a sense of meaninglessness and disconnection to one's identity. However, there is a counteremotion to guilt, that can reveal one's past as it was, without viewing through a leftist lens, without influence of ulterior political motives or an incomplete mapping of one's understanding, and should counteract this contrived guilt with a sense of wrongdoing. This being anger. The fact that who they are, their identity, has been denied to them to fulfill the masturbatory ivory tower delusions of grandeur of a few sanctimonious intellectuals, is far from just in any sense of the term.

People have a right to an unpoliticized view of their history. But, of course, history is written by the victors, and, without a shadow of a doubt, the prevailing culture and institutions is exclusively dominated by the political left. When people realize just what has been done to their culture and their history, the anger very quickly burns away the guilt that has been foisted upon them.

Tolerance – with the exception of tolerance towards anything grounded in the non-progressive – has been extended to things, groups, people, whose existence reveals itself as antithetical to progress. The bizarre cosying up to Islam – a considerably unprogressive ideology – from the progressive left fits neatly with one moral schema, that being the progressive stack. There can be tolerance for a hurried social liberalization under the banner of progress, even if it flirts with socially taboo topics – drag kids and pedophilia, for example. There cannot be any tolerance for anything remotely associated with views or lifestyles which are outside of the progressive sphere. Anything conservative-sounding must be shunned. Traditional Western morals must be discarded like a flaming brown paper bag of dog poop. These moralities are what keep individuals from fulfilling their potentials and self-actualization. Without them, the world would be more equitable, fair, happy, and utopian. Disgust for them, as an inhibiting force in society, is what appears to be just. The narratives and metanarratives behind the prevailing socially-accepted politics are what trigger feelings of tolerance, masked by a superficial 'love'; whereas naysayers and skeptics are the ones mired by 'hate'. Words, such as 'love' and 'hate', have been repurposed and almost redefined to describe certain natural emotional extremes, but within a context to promote or demote certain views according to how much of a fuss the talking heads have made over a certain politically lucrative event or cause. Disgust is a political antidote to the sickness of tolerance. Extreme tolerance is the political manifestation of a lack of convictions greater than oneself. Not only do certain causes, perhaps unthinkable a few generations ago – abortion, drag kids, open borders, sexually explicit pride parades, pedosexuality – have to be tolerated, but also adored. Disgust is a measured counteremotion to the forced narratives rammed down the throats of millions of apolitical Americans. Many so-called 'normies' reject the op-eds they've been subjected to, as their instinctual disgust reaction is often too strong for the forced tolerance to work.

These are the two salient emotions/counteremotions in the internet-dominated political circus: guilt-anger, tolerance-disgust. I have chosen these to illustrate how they can be used interchangeably to further a political narrative – and be inverted as a means to deepen one's position of power. Our current political circus isn't dictated by facts, logic, and reason, but preconditioned emotion. Sadly, emotion is more important than reason – especially in a democracy. A fiery orator, cunning rhetorician, or hopeful optimist can garner winning support in spite of a potentially hollow message or impending failure. What matters is emotion and comfort. Instilling guilt can pacify an electorate into stomaching policies contrary to their best interests.

The same applies with tolerance: not only can you ram injurious policies down the throat of the electorate but they'll love it, think they're intellectuals, pressure others into their position. The post-truth world is one where truth is a feeling according to the education, information, and narrative one imbibes. If, say, somebody has only been drip fed prevailing socially-accepted politics, they may be preconditioned to feel disdain towards anything the Narrative Complex condemns. Articles urging people to go by their feelings, their instincts, indicates that one cannot fully abandon their comfortable beliefs in favor of emotionless fact-based rhetoric. People tend to be more responsive to anecdotes, a story, a telos, rather than a volley of statistics presenting a differing, morally incorrect, worldview. Academia often frames study within a politically-loaded paradigm. Alien points of views are often given no unbiased treatment – if they're given treatment at all. Politically incorrect academics such as Charles Murray, Hans Hermann Hoppe, and Richard Duchesne have experienced discrimination for their failure to pay obeissance to the monolith of progress. Within universities, there is a social pressure for almost everybody to graduate in order to avoid becoming a failure. As a result, there's greater demand for apprentices and trade schoolers, on the one hand, and, a reduction of the quality of students, on the other. Due to this increased demand for university courses, many of them which have little significant real-world value outside of a narrow field of study have mushroomed. Politically-loaded courses have been created and offered to meet the demand. Of course, with the exception of purely academic STEM fields, the majority of courses – even STEM, in some cases – have been injected with leftist interpretations; calling into question the good faith and credibility of these courses. Students are often raised in an environment where there is no exposure to non-progressive views: going to daycare, kindergarten, school, and college; having liberal parent(s); watching mainstream media/TV, etc. Education often doesn't endow students with the ability to think critically given Academia's ideological unanimity. Try getting peer reviewed if your views are right of center. Over in the UK, a recent case steeped in double standards was when Cambridge researcher Noah Carl was fired over mildly right-wing views; but Cambridge lecturer Priyamvada Gopal was promoted merely hours after several grossly anti-white tweets, with the university supporting her views as "freedom of expression." Thomas Sowell pointed out how feeling has been confused with thinking. Sowell's thoughts could be perfectly captured by the NPC meme to be discussed in detail in a later chapter. Moreover, given the Media's ability to whip up a frenzy, darting from one manufactured outrage to the next, keeping the public in a perpetual mob-like state of injustice. The Media won't just tell you how to think, but how to feel. This is how the Media can be so persistently effective in influencing elections within the laughable charade called a democracy. The Narrative Complex can shape consumer demands to fatten profit margins; the Narrative Complex can shape voter preferences according to feeling, instead of impartially covering policy.

WHICH WAY? LEFT... OR RIGHT?

*"Politicians are the lowest form of life on earth.
Liberal Democrats are the lowest form
of politicians."*
—General George S. Patton

SOME MAY SAY THAT the left-right dichotomy is defunct, utterly useless. Granted, given the leftward shifts of the Overton Window, the idea of the left-wing or right-wing is only useful within a certain point in time. However, there are some fundamentally leftist and rightist principles which withstand the course of time and the nature of progress. Aside from economics, the inane big government vs small government debate is losing its significance as many young right wingers demand something greater than a diminutive government. Economics fails to play much of a significant role anymore. The Supply Side, Chicago School, Austrian School vs all stripes of Keynesianism and Marxist economics debate doesn't captivate the hearts of many. One of the many democratic problems of the right – with the exception of Trump – has been the question concerning political energy. The left is able to create, harness, and deploy rage banks of political energy, stoked up by some great perceived injustice – oftentimes inequality of some description – to inspire would-be voters to get up and vote. The left is youthful and still symbolizes a young purpose to many which will grant it perpetual political motion as long as: 1) democracy is the dominant political order 2) a relative degree of religiosity exists 3) society remains heterogeneous and 4) any conceivable form of inequality remains visible within society. Of course, barring the first point – democracy – the latter three points will always exist in some form because people are not equal. Politicians will command rage banks until the end of time. The point is: economics, deregulation, and marginal tax cuts will not inspire political action – injustice will. And for that reason, The so-called 'Groyper Wars' reveal a threatening metapolitical force to the powers that be: they cannot be appeased by their lily livered solutions. Those embodied by the Groyper meme want something mere economics cannot offer. They are homesick for a land and time they never knew; just a fading memory falling out of public consciousness. The Groypers feel conned by the deceased political representatives who approved the demographic change of their country, and by the politicians and groups who supposedly represent them, but attempt to have them silenced while mockingly endorsing individuals and policies antithetical to their ends. The Groypers feel like they've been done a great injustice. And, because of this, they have a rage bank full of energy, ready to be unleashed.

To be brief, some eternal signifiers of leftism and rightism are as follows:

Leftism:
- egalitarianism
- man outside of nature
- social justice
- globalism
- acceptance instead of overcoming
- liberalism
- materialism
- linear time/progressive or whig theory of history

Rightism:
- hierarchy
- man within nature
- personal responsibility
- regionalism/nationalism
- self-improvement
- illiberalism
- order
- religion/the transcendental
- eternal time/cyclical view of history

If we were to analyze a mainstream conservative group such as Turning Point USA, everything they stand for is traditionally leftist. One of the most wicked tricks was to prioritize a quasi-religious devotion of free market capitalism as the right's position. With the exception of 'self-improvement' –

which, to a certain degree, can be vitiated due to the enhancement of technological progress thanks to capitalism; stifling the individual's drive – all traditionally rightist positions are debased and subverted by the real-world expression of free market capitalism. Furthermore, the real-world expression of free market capitalism has done more to advance traditionally leftist positions into the world's mind than communism ever did. And, besides, revolutions aren't cheap – the money had to come from somewhere. Funnily enough, the left – being classically anticapitalist – and the new/dissident right – being contemporarily anticapitalist – both reject capitalism, but for different reasons. Any overlap which can be obtained between the two groups often reaches an impasse for differing reasons. Sadly classical leftism is a reaction to post-Enlightenment liberalism and is only grounded to its materialism. This is why it will only ever act as a school of remora fish sucking on the main liberal body. Mainstream conservatism is merely a defunct branch of liberalism, but one that is tarred with the same "Nazi" brush. In fact, any slight deviation from progressive dogma is grounds for "Nazism." According to many on the left, Harry Potter author J.K. Rowling qualifies as a "Nazi" for her anti-transgender, pro-old-school-feminist views. She can wholeheartedly agree with every single other progressive talking point, but this single disagreement is sufficient grounds for cancellation. Anybody who isn't unabashedly progressive/neoliberal – and these points can be used interchangeably in social policy, despite nuanced and grandly unimportant differences in an economic realm – is categorized as "hateful." Those who blaspheme against the progressive Cathedral indulge in "hate speech." All non-progressive views are automatically discredited as "hate." If you control all institutions, it's very easy to secure power if you simply delegitimize any challengers by denigrating their words and actions. To add, it's even easier to secure power if you have billions of dollars sloshing around to help disseminate your narratives, making them an irreplaceable mainstay within public consciousness through lifelong brainwashing in the Narrative Complex.

Without the globalist tendencies of the real-world expression of free market capitalism, global communications, and, by extension, the Narrative Complex, couldn't cement its grip in controlling the flow of their information. The importance of monopolizing the flow of information cannot be stressed enough. Big money dictates what is true and what is not. The age of reason has managed to take us in an anti-human direction. Material progress and economics dictates all prevailing globalized values. Money is the global lingo. Money makes the world go wrong. When money is involved, there's no real need for interpreters. Flows are the way of the 21st Century world: flows of money, flows of resources, flows of labor, flows of capital, flows of immigrants, you name it. Perhaps a dichotomy of rationalism vs instinct can be invoked. On the one hand, rationalism is what has civilized barbarians and ushered in this great epoque of tremendous wealth where the average person can splurge on an iPhone and gorge on a Big Mac.

Instincts leave us mired in savagery. One of the key features of a materialist world has been the abandonment of human instinct in favor of rationalism. Instincts are a throwback to an undeveloped humanity, placed far down on an evolutionary chain in linear time. Rationalism is the goal and because instincts are observably irrational they must be suppressed. The Independent even ran an article detailing how the use of magnets can disable parts of the brain to rid oneself of religiosity and xenophobia. The apotheosis of man requires losing his primordial humanity as there's no room for him in the rational framework. Within the rational framework, time takes on a different meaning. Time, apart from a linear view, becomes a yardstick to document human progress. For the individual, time begins and ends with their own life. Observability is key within a rationalist paradigm. What happens after death is no concern of yours – you won't be there to see it!

As I illustrated in my debut book, "A Matter of Time," the concept of time preference is one of the overriding principles in any healthy society which sees itself as a going concern. One of the central rifts between the material and the transcendental is either group's conception of time. This is not always clear cut, but a distinction can be made between the two. Within the materialist framework, the concept of time is a social construct. It is only to be lived once, and to be lived well with whatever is at the individual's disposal. History is teleology, working toward an ideal on a linear plane. It must become humanity's duty to aim for goals prescribed by our intellectual betters and anointed elites who will guide use to an ideal. In a way, the fatalist view of the end of history is already upon us. But, when we've reached sufficient material wealth, comfort, intellect, tolerance, understanding, secularization – what then? Life is littered with struggle. Struggle is what impels somebody to get out of bed in the morning. Struggle, within reason, endows somebody with a purpose. What happens when society becomes struggle-free? What happens when rational man cannot rationalize anymore? We've already seen symptoms of this fatal disease rock many urban areas. People begin to fill their lives with empty experiences to plaster over the seventy-year spell of boredom between cradle to grave. People don't want to have children anymore. In part, it's because of 'the economy'; however, this is a cop out. Throughout the entire rest of human history, conditions were far worse, and people still managed to afford to have kids. Anti-natalism is perhaps the most pernicious indictment of the neoliberal world. Despite all the material progress and scientific triumphs, people evaluate the world and sometimes themselves to be too defective to reproduce.

To somebody who appreciates the transcendental, time assumes an eternal nature, unbound to human apprehensions or mischaracterizations. Time is eternal. Civilizations are cyclical. To this mode of thinking, life goes on and on and on after one perishes. Even if there is no afterlife on a transcendental level, one's children – and nation, by extension – are the continuation of life into the future, beyond one's physical life. Those whose view of time is eternal, rather than a construct, will tend to forgo present consumption in favor of future gain – whatever form it assumes. Here is one of the major spiritual, metapolitical, and lifestyle differences between the left and right. Meaning and time are indissolubly linked. Things which don't conform to a lengthy or implied longevity don't take on much significance in the grand scheme of things. Progress seeks to improve general conditions within a framework of linear time, whereas ideologies based on transcendental ideas seek to endure the so-called "test of time." Progress is prisoner to its own conception of temporariness – and is, therefore, destined to fail the test of time. Other self-evident principles, such as the concept of the nation, are innately and indelibly ingrained, withstanding all forms of propaganda. Transcendental principles can't be assigned monetary value via the price system, and, in the current world, cannot be rationalized or empirically observed. Many are left scratching their heads and even mock those who believe in such irrational tripe. But, in many cases, those esteemed rationalist headscratchers forgo a legacy beyond their own life; in other words, rationalism has drifted so far from instinct it has forgotten how to "person." Nationalism, in particular, cannot be fully rationalized under liberal metrics or epistemology. Frankly, nationalism is an irrational concept during times of great prosperity: how can you assign a higher value to your own kind over others? But, when the proverbial hits the fan, who can you trust? Would you trust those who look like you, talk like you, have a shared history, purpose, culture, sense of humor, and experiences, or somebody else? Another fatal flaw is the instinctual amnesia; placing oneself above the limitations of humanity, wanting to leave humanity behind but forgetting animal instincts and biological imperatives. The belief in reason has put people above their own humanity. By abandoning instinct, life is inauthentic. People are not meant to be hyper-rational intellectually-ascended beings à la Sheldon from Big Bang Theory. Passion, instincts, and emotions predominate the lives of many. These are the people who will live on, as their hyper-rational counterparts reason themselves out of procreation. Something as basic as the emergence of conflict or human biodiversity, when constructing a multicultural society, is forgotten by many intelligent, rational people.

Something that is criminally unpopular is the correlation between lifestyles and political affiliation. People of certain lifestyles and philosophies tend to embrace certain political affiliations. For example, there's a higher likelihood that a God-fearing family man who lifts weights will vote for a right wing party than an overweight atheist green-haired single woman. Some political affiliations can be assumed by one's type of lifestyle. Those keen on self-improvement or discipline will be turned off by metapolitically left-wing social causes such as body positivity or fat acceptance. However, this crude schema makes an exception for those who reside in an upper-middle class left-wing milieu, as they probably have some form of higher education and have lived in a narrative bubble. Progressive views to affluent liberal types are all they know and have assumed a quasi-religious nature. To paraphrase an internet maxim: "the right thinks the left is wrong, the left thinks the right is evil." On the whole, there's little amicable overlap to be had in good-hearted political discussions – especially done online behind avatars and pseudonyms. But there seems to be a deeper, more metaphysical departure between supporters of both political wings. Sadly, in many cases, the differences between left and right often appear to be truly irreconcilable. But, I would contend that this is a feature, rather than a bug, within a secular liberal democracy. Returning to the rightist's predilection for hierarchy over equality – in the traditional left/right positions above – capitalism, as an inherently unequal economic order, wins the vote for the metapolitically rightist individual, since socialism promises equality. Liberal democracy, being materialist in nature, will subdivide society by preferred economic order as economics is the transcendental expression of materialism – how do you want it: equal and accepting (socialist); or unequal and overcoming (capitalist)? In America, the socialist/capitalist divide has been vacuously viewed as big government/small government, sucking all the nuance out of politicking. Voters are really spoilt for choice, here.

Following on from lifestyle and political affiliation, the saturation of popular culture with leftist overtones ensures one thing: popular culture aficionados are far likelier to support leftist politics and metapolitically leftist causes such as open borders. That's not to say the mainstream right isn't completely passive to open borders. But, the reasons for open borders differ: for the left, open borders facilitate refugees or those in need to seek sanctuary, raze obstacles to globalism, and gain a demographic-democratic advantage. For the right, open borders remove fetters to the international movement of capital and labor. Popular culture is merely a lifestyle-inspiring branch of the Narrative Complex, depicting as to how one should lead their lives, in dumbed-down messaging to reach the widest possible audience. This ties into creating the perfect producing-consumer. The producing-consumer who lives in a pod, gets chipped, feasts on bug meat, self-sterilizes, and whose life is dictated by brusque sporadic dopamine secretions when consuming product. Nominally atheistic, their religion is cummies. All they do is attempt to satisfy their insatiable worn-out dopamine receptors which have become more fried than the maggot burger patty they gobble down after commuting for 90 minutes in a cattle car. The person, Malvina Reynolds, behind the Little Boxes song was wrong; we won't live in little boxes, but pods. What we've kindly witnessed is a political fusion of liberalism. The left, right, big business, and the bulk of the electorate have been domesticated under the banner of liberalism. Man's 'Faustian spirit' is channeled and recoded for economic progress and production. The liberal system, preying upon the individual's self-interest and predisposition to having high time preferences, unites politics, business, and the personal under one neat liberal ontology. Liberalism subsumes everything. Every facet of daily life, every unconscious moment is saturated by left liberalism, in particular.

Liberalism is what keeps the system afloat. A God-fearing society isn't necessarily a consumerist society, but a liberalism-fearing society is consumerist by necessity. The vapid distractions offered by liberalism and the pallid fattening of profit margins – turned morally good by economists' metrics – don't quite satiate the soul. While modern enlightened society is enamored by their own materialist self-importance, those very materialists often fail to have children to pass on their ideological legacy. For this reason, institutions are co-opted to pass on the ideological legacy of those who have been frightfully termed by Ed Dutton as so-called "spiteful mutants."

But, if we were to analyze the system, the current consumerist society is no accident. The system, which has been propped up by Smithian self-interest and high time preferences, necessitates the continuance of self-debasing quests in chasing the dopamine dragon. Big money and lobbying groups petition the government in their own self-interest; politicians duly accept in their own self-interest; the electorate votes in their own self-interest – and what of the future? It can go to hell. Who cares? I delve further into the issue concerning politicians and high time preferences in 'A Matter of Time':

> *"As a stunning reflection of our age of high time preferences, our politicians often embody society at large. In this case, our politicians don't act for tomorrow, but for today. At the time of writing this, several Western leaders are childless. Some people may shrug their shoulders at this information, but what is their skin in the game? Why should they*

care what happens to their nations after they expire if they haven't left behind a legacy? Talk is cheap. Politics is dictated by hollow platitudes and big money. There needs to be something more substantial as a guarantee – collateral – to ensure that leaders don't figuratively screw the pooch. That is, to say, of course, that not all politicians who are childless don't care about the welfare of their countries once they've left office. Politicians with children often linger like a bad smell after their time in office to cement their family's stead and to continue to cheerily accept kickbacks from multinationals or other myriad interest groups to protect their political dynasty. The underlying pattern for most globalist politicians is either: 1) no skin in the game – childlessness or 2) protecting their skin in the game – prostituting themselves to major corporate interests.

For the childless politician, it doesn't really matter for his/her country to be flooded by unassimilable, hostile migrants, who, apart from humanity, share nothing in common with the host population. Flourishing as upstanding members of the community isn't a priority, especially as the existing incentive structures – welfare, housing, schooling, anti-racist activists, political correctness, etc – all act as impediments towards any semblance of integration. Furthermore, since large minorities can put forward their own political candidates, who, invariably "play the system" in order to command the most resources, laws, rights, perquisites for their own group; questions concerning the legitimacy of a political system, which allows legal elements alien to the founding national stock to become embedded within the nation's laws to benefit hostile minorities, should be made. Once the proverbial hits the fan, the childless politician will either have begun the process of ossification or be heavily guarded in a gated residence. Either way, they don't get to suffer the consequences of their own actions. The other politician with a legacy to protect will work assiduously to ensure their children and grandchildren never feel the consequences of their traitorous actions. The underlying theme appears to be the democratization or socialization of consequences onto others. The populace will feel the brunt of the consequences for impulsive economic and immigration policies – not the politician. It is the working class who have been hardest hit by feel-good, jazzhands, Kumbaya globalism. How else could the spiritual bleakness of the current political landscape be cloaked? How else can millions of voters gingerly follow the neoliberal Pied Piper? A cross between fantastical promises of a prosperous utopian world, and viciously silencing or smearing naysayers, has been the favored ingredient to the neoliberal melting pot. The working class – not city-dwelling elites – have been alienated by deindustrialization and mass immigration. Their communities have been kneecapped by joblessness, crime, addiction, suicide, broken homes – the root causes of which can be, in a large part, attributed to a spiritual decay which has been repackaged as dopamine-secreting feel-good politics promoted by the Narrative Complex."

Those involved only wish to get theirs before the ship goes down. Besides, the Narrative Complex will always be there to protect the system's interest – the audience's attention span is short, and, additionally, a lot of the audience places religious devotion on the sludge-like message pumped out by the Narrative Complex. People can go around pretending to be a big-brained, high-IQ individual, after half-memorizing the latest NYT column on why an obscure trade deal is beneficial to the world's economy, while drearily repeating tired buzzwords to condemn atavistic white flyover-country-dwellers tired with deindustrialization. The same people champion economic views disingenuously packaged under "limited government," when, in actuality, serve to bring about their demographic displacement and politico-economic disenfranchisement.

Ironically, a glimpse into the future of America would resemble urban California at the current pace. Millions have expressed a desire to abandon the state due to its prohibitively expensive cost of living, unsanitary conditions, promotion of aggressively progressive politics, illegal immigration, demographic shift, and a myriad of other reasons. The widespread flight from California transcends political lines. As California's urban areas are overwhelmingly liberal, when Californians leave the state, they take their idealistic politics with them, then implement them in whichever new – inevitably red – state they now call home. While taking advantage of low rates of crime and taxes, some rise to positions of power to force their ideals upon the rest of the state. In a matter of time, that new state begins to resemble California –

aside from the paradisal beaches, perfect climate, and rugged terrain. Look at Colorado and Nevada now, and then Idaho and Montana in the future. These states will become unrecognizable. But the problem remains: liberalism follows Californians wherever they go. They simply refuse to interrogate their own worldview, ignoring the fact that in the space of a little over three decades, California went from the envy of the world to a third world dump due to their leftist policies. That die hard liberals wish to leave their beloved state is a subtle vote of no confidence in their ideas, even though it's not verbalized. They can't wait to escape the consequences of their policies, only to be granted another chance at enacting their worldview somewhere quieter and quainter. But, despite the will of many Californians to leave their state, another, more sinister, pattern has emerged among more militant liberal types. Although they have become conscious of the disastrous consequences of their policies; like locusts, they wish to move onto greener pastures to despoil. And here is what the mainstream conservative fails to grasp: the liberal seeks to hold and maintain power no matter the consequences, while the conservative only seeks to cling onto his principles like a koala to a towering eucalyptus tree in a roaring forest fire. Sadly, for the mainstream conservative, power will trump principles every single time. Strangely enough, the insistence to cling onto outdated principles is partly what renders them ineffective in the long term. Although neoliberals look askance at Mainstream American conservative principles; in essence, those principles are a form of political self-sterilization.

They hemorrhage political energy to fruitless causes, instill apathy to their desired ends, and act like a greyhound on a racetrack chasing an unreachable decoy, while the country becomes a less free, favelafied strip mall. America is a beautiful country with wonderful people – that is worth conserving; GDP-obsessed, consumerist multicultural nihilism, however, is not. Although this may sound "out-there," one of the reasons why some many young people are depressed and underwhelmed with life is because they know nothing of import worth dying for. Nobody would die for neoliberalism and 3% growth. Likewise, nobody would die for consumer goods, unless they're extremely damaged.

Labor has devolved into a pastime – in the literal sense of the world: to pass the time – until consumption comes around to take the edge of everyday life. Many millennials don't have a family to come home to after a long day of desk-jockeying or performing some aimless service job designed to whittle away the hours before death. Labor itself isn't directed to any constructive ends. The average person never interacts with the direct fruits of their labor, and performs their labor with the assistance of technology or a labor-saving device to enhance productivity, turning labor into an indirect exercise. From an ontological standpoint, the laborer isn't really *there* when they do their work. Labor is conducted via proxies, furthering the individual worker from reality. And, when the laborer commutes home, often by a lengthy journey to an unpleasantly diminutive shoebox apartment, the laborer seeks to spend their meager remuneration on distractions from reality – since they probably cannot afford a family if they live in a major city. Leisure time often characterizes the individual. Archetypes that I will explain later in this book, such as the consoomer and AWFL, embody the kind of person who would splurge their disposable income on frivolities like alcohol, fast food, and dopamine-teasing experience to dull the pain of an existence they misconceive. Is their life really life if it is lived vicariously through technological proxies? They do, they are, nothing authentic. In fact, their lives and identities are marked by a militant will to live as inauthentically as possible. And a metacultish mentality is erected around modern urban life. They live as a last man; self-deprecation is their calling. They seek solace in self-sterilization, ethnomasochism, and dopamine-inducing virtue signaling in progressive politics. Their lives are almost one giant copepost in justifying their unlived existence.

Things aren't much better in the countryside. In the American's relegation from human being to interchangeable economic unit, a semblance of stability is lost. You could be flying high in April, but shot down in May. The working class has been sold out by their political and trade representatives in favor of globalism and 90 genders. Their jobs have been offshored to benefit megacorporations. Their neighborhoods cease to resemble the place they call home. The quality of their children's schools has nosedived. They were probably close to somebody who battled and lost to some form of drug addiction – which, of course, is manufactured by unscrupulous megacorporations. Several industries have been relocated overseas. The instability of life becomes truly revealed: maybe tomorrow their status as American economic unit is made redundant over less profitable wage rates. In the city, the fruits of one's labor are often concealed by the dominance of the service industry, and, in the country, the fruits of one's labor in manufacturing may be meaningless when the local industry either moves abroad or is no longer competitive against offshoring megacorporations who enjoy diversified supply chains and economies of scale.

Down political lines, although correlation doesn't equal causation, allegiance to political parties, as a generalization, could be identified through types of employment. In 2016, deindustrialized manufacturing communities voted overwhelmingly for Trump. However, those with higher levels of education tend to remain in urban areas and work in service based jobs, which partly explains as to why the educated person favored Clinton over Trump. Those who received higher levels of education were left to stew in a cauldron of progressive thought. But another, more politically incorrect factor, which has been correctly identified by some publications, was the fact that Trump's election was thanks to the white lower and middle classes in America. Folks with higher levels of education are likelier to earn higher incomes which affords the high income earner a greater degree of freedom to escape the consequences of progressive politics and to remain within the coastal elitist bubble. Lower and middle America live the reality of 55 years of progressive politics; particularly a melange of lax immigration controls and neoliberal economics. Every interchangeable economic unit has a price tag. Family life across the board has become vitiated to favor production. The dream of a stay-at-home mother taking care of the family, while the father wins the bacon, is a distant memory. Production is restricted when only half of the adults within the household are empowered enough to pursue a career. Separating the family is a necessary step to ensure maximum production – on paper. However, in reality, raw productivity hasn't necessarily increased as much as boasted. A large portion of jobs created to accommodate the tsunami of female labor entering the workforce contemporaneously to the various social revolutions of the 60s has led to the creation of spurious forms of employment. One of the triumphs of women's liberation, aside from beefing up economic stats, has been to create a more consumerist society. Instead of saving for the kids, a house, car, education, and so on, stagnant funds have been freed to slosh around as disposable income intended for consooming product. The dissolution of the American family has been nothing short of criminal. The consequences have led to a society bereft of a proper upbringing, guidance, and purpose, reflected in their lifestyle choices. All of these social revolutions have confluenced, following over two generations of overtly progressive social dominance, in what appears to be a political powder keg. Some may look askance at the following pronouncement, but there appears to be a political butting-of-heads which has assumed the form of something more metaphysical.

CHAPTER
5

WOKE CAPITAL

"Imagine having the same politics as Burger King and Pepsi and thinking you're a revolutionary or a dissident."
—Genie, Twitter User

"We live in a world where there is more and more information, and less and less meaning."
—Jean Baudrillard

What is Woke?

WOKE. Woke is to be awakened to subtler, nuanced, politics on the hard left side of the aisle. To be woke is to be on the left of progress. To be woke is to reject heteronormativity (where heterosexual pair-bonded couples are the norm), whiteness, eurocentrism, imperialism, -phobias, -isms, socially constructed hierarchies, etc. Social Justice Warriors often consider themselves 'woke', but being 'woke' goes beyond mere social justice. To be woke is to claim a heightened state of social consciousness, a new post-enlightenment enlightenment deconstructing most pre-existing pro-Western norms. While there is a definite intellectual energy behind 'wokeness', to identify woke capital would be to apply hard left politics to big business. Weird, huh? Not really. The post-new left has unenthusiastically decried modern capitalism as megacorporations have become something of an unexpected ally – considering how big business and capitalism have, for generations, been inextricably linked with the right. Big business (capitalism) and wokeness (communism/socialism with a 21st Century twist) are both materialist philosophies. It follows that two materialist philosophies – big business and wokeness – would oust former, more metaphysical values associated with the right who are socially seen as being 'uncool', in favor of parenting a more materialist synthesis in the form of "Woke Capital." The main point to remember is that so-called "Woke Capital" under any other conditions could be described as a left-wing form of capitalism. Capitalism is often associated with the right, and for this reason, some may split hairs saying that the very rightist essence of capitalism precludes it from being remotely left wing. However, the overtly leftist social nature of modern megacorporation capitalism is undeniable.

After slowly breaching public consciousness to become consumerist mainstays through relentless product placement, advertisement, and now from dipping their toes to cannonballing into leftward ho! politics, major corporations have gamed politics to their favor to bring about a society which would be more likely to consume. A neoliberal economy – a global economy – necessitates the erasure of borders to facilitate flows of capital and labor; the homogenization of culture, language, and goals; the dampening of history, religion, and political energy; and, eventually, a global shift of consciousness away from the spiritual, romantic, and sentimental to be replaced by behaviors which would be conducive to profit maximization. Identity is a thing of the past. Plus, you wouldn't want to be deemed to be a 'hateful' bigot identitarian. Sadly, for most, identity is a fundamental part of being. Identity provides purpose, meaning, history, significance, direction, and a future worth preserving. Identity acts as a moor, a starting point, something desperately needed in a postmodern world bereft of objective meaning. Identity provides the individual with the ability to decode an increasingly technological, narrative-dominated, and subjective world dogged by infinite groups vying for power. By denying people their identity – in this case, a historical identity linked to nationhood and religion – an identity must be forged by different means. As hollowed out individuals, whose history is maliciously maligned by the Narrative Complex, family life deglamorized, religion desacralized, and social life turned into little more than superficial hedonistic interactions – this is where brands step in; this is where brands become identities, themselves. Brands symbolize recognizable logos, social status, wealth, belonging, taste, desires to almost transcend an ethnoreligious level. It's no coincidence that those with an atheistic outlook are more likely to self-identify with a brand. Conspicuous consumerism can denote class or socioeconomic status where content of character can't. For society to be more receptive to consumerism or materialism, a sense of purpose and belief in ends greater than oneself must be cheapened to the point where their intrinsic worth is lower than the allure of consumerism. Individual values must be rearranged to prioritize present minded gratification over irreplaceable values which cannot be assigned monetary value. In the so-called 'Information Age', information can be crafted to benefit people at the expense of others. The ability to receive information via smartphone, tablet, laptop, etc, is often lauded as a good in itself – with the exception of the dissemination of 'hate speech' – without appraising the value, veracity, or intentions of the circulating information received or promoted by these mediums. Corporations aren't simply just productive forces anymore: they have rapidly become supercharged political energies, too. Money in advertisement, lobbying, and causes which can influence the Narrative Complex's positioning can be employed to tweak the public's desire into viewing and valuing branded consumer goods more favorably, not only from a consumer's perspective, but also a moral one. Progressive politics, in recent years, have positioned themselves as a moral yardstick in the vacuum left behind by a weakened Christianity and a West suffering from low self-esteem, offering no suitable replacement. By adopting a quasi-religious unwritten moral framework, corporations can represent themselves as just moral crusaders, supporting every civil rights movement, social quest, or cause once it's socially safe to do so. During the process of legalizing gay marriage, most major corporations were nowhere to be seen backing this cause. However, fast forward a few years, and a significant portion of major corporations incorporate a rainbow flag into their brand logo to virtue signal their support for Pride Month. Corporations such as Dr Pepper and KLM have also expressed their support for LGBT+ with implicitly sexual advertisements. Sex does, after all, sell. Other corporations have gone a step further in expressing their support for non-binaries – those whose gender doesn't match up with the male-female binary. A decade ago, this enthusiastic support would've been unimaginable, let alone the mainstreaming of Gender Theory; hitherto practically unknown to the general public. The bottom line is that major corporations can play a role in adjusting the public consciousness through clumsy political posturing, advertisement, and promoting narratives which contribute towards creating a more materialist society – to their own benefit.

There is very much an emphasis on promoting the "real you" so long as it neatly fits within an ontologically progressive-slash-consumerist paradigm. But who is the real you? Authenticity is taken away from underneath us as the Narrative Complex has redefined truth as exclusively subjective, varying from person to person. One may identify as they please, as long as it isn't right wing or straight, white, and male. Those problematic truths are to be denied. That's just, like, your opinion, man. If the whole framework dictating reality itself is overhauled to be repackaged into serving political narrative, then is the way you identify really who you are, or who you're expected to be? If you have been denied an unrevised version of your history, a dysfunctional upbringing as part as a modern social experiment in keeping with progressive values, is the secular deracinated consumer really you?

Establishment Conservatives, RINOs, Neolibs, Boomercons, etc, all champion marginal jumps in the DOW and GDP, and falls in tax rates as movement towards an abstraction of a free market economy. We mustn't disappoint the holy line on the graph. However, particularly in the case of the bulk of mainstream conservatives, much of this support for tax cuts, deregulation, and less state intervention is in order to bring about a fantasized goal of 'limited government'. Unfortunately, for them, limited government has been a fancy exercise in futility for over a hundred years. A more multicultural, expansive, energetic, populous, pluralistic, atomized, and materialist America will require more government presence to mediate and unify myriad conflicting ends – not to mention the newly imported population with a penchant for more socialistic welfare programs, with a right to vote. Despite conservatives continuing to support corporations with quasi-libertarian fervor, corporations have both openly and brazenly adopted progressive social positions designed to affront or undermine dying conservative values. From another perspective, it can be argued that a more laissez-faire economic approach is the most powerful generator of social change – if so-called 'conservative values' are worth keeping. It can also be argued that the Protestant work ethic, Dutch/British laissez-faire, and the Industrial Revolution are a materialist by-product of Rome's loss of power and influence in Northwest Europe between the 16th to 17th Century. Without a shadow of a doubt, the best functioning, most productive, and efficient economy would be one with least state interference. However, from a social perspective, it would be ruinous to traditions, morality, epistemology, language, nationhood, spirit, and customs – especially in its present form where megacorporations have the ability to shape public consciousness to their own profiteering advantage. The growth of technology, the abundance, the falling costs and waiting times to sate one's material desires have led wider society to abandon former customs in favor of immediate gratification. Information and technology has been a game-changer. A simple hands-off approach and limited government won't cut it anymore. The toothpaste is out of the tube. Everyone has information at the tip of their fingers, limitless desires, and their opinions all matter. Of course, if the wider public were more traditional in their outlook, a 'free market' economy would yield different products, at first, as the demands of this public wouldn't be as vapid or have the need to fill a void with meaningless consumer goods. However, if corporations had the ability to effect change by influencing major institutions to weaken the fabric of that society, for temporary gain, then, as the market is a consumer-driven economy, it would be beneficial to alter the way consumers think. For conservatives, it is understandable to see the alignment of free-market principles with the mainstream right given their generations-old fight against communism and socialism. Sadly, for them, the enemy has evolved and they're tilting at windmills. Modern corporations have cleverly synthesized the right's predilection for entrepreneurship, enterprise, wealth-creation, and a semblance of hierarchy, with foisting a potent progressive cultural bent on society. Furthermore, it keeps conservatives fighting within a materialist paradigm, which, in itself, is an admittance of defeat. By merely accepting economic – or materialist – attempted refutations of leftism – which few persons of import gave a damn about and no real-life application – conservatives have shied away from fighting a cultural battle, in recent years, which the very corporations they defend undermine. Aside from the social change promoted by megacorporations, they can also lobby the state to enact fiscal and monetary policies to their own benefit which jostle smaller companies out of the market. Traditionally moderate left-wing economic policies such as minimum wage and tax hikes hamper productivity and profitability of smaller companies who will struggle to compete against megacorporations. The bigger they are, the easier they can suffer tax burdens overseas, automate low-skilled occupations, and undercut competition in tighter regional markets by skilfully lowering profit margins, enjoy economies of scale, and claim an almost monopolist status artificially vivified by state interference. A genuine return to a limited government would be unfeasible under the current political structure since it would add unnecessary competition to megacorporations. If a politician were to run on a limited government ticket, they would never secure adequate financial backing unless they were a billionaire. Even then, though, what if this hypothetical billionaire Ron Paul type were to secure power? He would be hamstrung by a myriad of private interests and the so-called "Swamp," preventing him from ending the Fed, dismantling the Military Complex or Narrative Complex, or anything else without risking his life. Besides, a gradualist approach to shrinking the size of the federal government would lead to short-term unemployment of the establishment's most loyal supporters, only to be undone when the next politician is elected into office. Could you imagine the armies of DMV diversity hires or overweight bitter Karens clamoring about having to get a private sector role? Impossible. Too many people are wholly dependent on the system's largesse as is, anyway. There would need to be a shift in focus away from the reductive small vs big government model as that battle was lost a long time ago. While your dear author isn't the biggest fan of so-called "big government," the federal government has been co-opted to reinforce the worst, most parasitical incentive structures imaginable.

If we were to analyze the self-detonating nature of right-wing social views and economic (that being materialist and free market) views, the two cannot co-exist from a purely material framework – aside from big capital's need for a frivolous, consumerist, and largely godless society to reap the greatest benefit. Although early phases of investment required for aggregate low time preferences to prevail within the investor, technology annihilates many incentive structures forcing low time preferences due to the readily available status of most goods and products without requiring the deferral of gratification. Technique, à la Ellul, forces individuals to live vicariously through technology. The process of continuous improvement – technique – simplifies everything to a point where man himself is obsolescent. Technique simplifies the banalest of human interactions into undesirable wastes of time, tugging away at the fabric of society. This, in turn, is complemented by the atomization inherent within a multicultural society. Time preferences are raised to the point where waiting is for losers. Without aggregate low time preferences, society fails to become a going concern. Everyone lives for today – just like John Lennon's 'Imagine:' everyone is reduced to an infantilized, responsibility-shirking hedonist with no concerns beyond their immediate enjoyment.

As I point out in 'A Matter of Time':'

"Returning back to John Lennon's Imagine, what would happen if everyone were to be 'living for today'? Who'd worry about tomorrow? Somebody has to. Our children will pick up the tab for our actions, if we're not too careful. If we consumed like locusts, what will be left after we're gone – and I'm not just talking about consumption in general, what of the nations our ancestors built: the architecture, the art, the culture, the blood shed, the lives lost, the turmoil, strife, and hardship endured so that we could enjoy a safe and luxurious (decaying) civilization? It's not too hard to imagine – we're seeing its decline in real time. Rome declined gradually for around 10-15 generations before it eventually fell. The West is in an uncannily similar process of decline, perhaps accelerated by the accessibility of technology and unprecedented levels

of wealth creation which sedates the individual from the realization of many social ills. Consumerism blinkers the individual from distress. Almost like a local anaesthetic, that needs to be constantly reapplied to dull the pain of modern life; people don't want to look up from the consumerist feeding trough to see the impending dangers wrought by their selfish, self-deifying, vapid lifestyles. Many may see the problems conceived by their passivity and selfishness, but figure they'll be six-foot under by the time their chickens come home to roost. Their lives burn up quicker than a shooting star, and, like a shooting star, their memory will enjoy a similar lifespan. They wish not to suffer the consequences of their actions, avoiding guilt by materialist distractions, which, in turn, sets in motion a decivilizing piranha-like voracity to satiate their multiple galloping desires. And in a similar piranha-like fashion, those who purely live by high time preferences relegate their behaviors to something more animal, primitive, carnal, rather than civil."

The sad reality is, the immutable laws of supply and demand have become revolutionary drivers for social change. Individuals and small businesses who fail to genuflect at the altar of progress must face the wrath of thousands of potential consumers armed with Twitter and Instagram accounts calling for your cancellation. Advertisement, influencers, actors, e-celebs all pique consumer demand, while espousing non-progressive views forces that demand to evaporate. Capitalism has done more to further leftism in the past 50 years than leftism could ever dream of. The sheer genius of wielding power from a board room of wealthy neoliberal apparatchiks. We still have kangaroo courts, in the form of internet mobs. Execution is no longer hosted on a scaffold in a public setting; now, your execution is termination from employment, the public setting is the indelible mark left by your name on every major search engine. The whole world will know you once uttered "all lives matter" loud enough for the snivelling soon-to-be spinster in the HR department to hear while she eavesdropped as she made her instant coffee. Corporations create their own demand through the religion of progress. Imagine, if you will, a world where televangelists are considered cool trendsetters to tens of millions of impressionable young people itching to one-up each other on how progressive they are? In no time, these televangelists peddling consumerist snake oil would be multi-billionaires. By adopting a quasi-Trotskyist permanent revolution, chasing down every last inequality – which, by the way, will always exist through necessity to remain relevant – corporations can drive their own demand by capitalizing on the religious zeal emanating from young progressives and low-information normies too terrified to be outed as "racist" for their apathy.

Woke corporations have slyly tapped into the vanity of youngsters by virtue signaling a plethora of causes, mostly surrounding the LGBT+ 'community'. These causes match up with the moral compass of the younger generations. Their preferred brands – filling in for their lost sense of received identity – can also strike chords by resonating with their preferred politics, which has become a moral framework etched into the hearts and minds of many through education and narratives, metanarratives, storylines, etc, promoted by the media. Corporations have become, in part, moral arbiters in the current year. Not only do corporations answer to your consumer demands, but have been ordained as a contemporary priestly caste lining their pockets via a modernized sale of indulgences. By ideologically siding with the more energetic, tech-savvy, vain, materialistic younger generations, corporations can expect free advertisement through the use of social media where the happy consumer proudly displays their branded consumer goods for the rest of their peers. Imitation, being the greatest form of flattery, and, people being social animals craving belonging, will go along with their preferred social media influencers or group of friends in both purchasing consumer goods and deferring to the accompanying political views. Those who consume are associated with being 'cool'. Those who aren't cool thereby become pariahs by default, by rejecting brands and their accompanying politics. But, it doesn't stop there. It isn't just implicit when it comes to manufacturing consent. Alarmingly, corporations have sided with governments to form an unholy alliance where the electorate is stripped of their incomes for the exchange of often useless or harmful consumer goods. Big Tech, in particular, has been immersed in several scandals where they have been accused of tampering with algorithms to further their preferred political causes and even directly colluding with governments to suppress 'fake news' – alternative news sources contradicting the mainstream media's narratives – and handing over the information of social media users to the relevant authorities if they use 'hate speech' on their platforms. If you don't like it, you can start your own X, Y, or Z company – they're a private company, they can do whatever they want. Although megacorporations have, on the whole, fundamentally abandoned American values, it doesn't stop mainstream conservatives from supporting them – or what they've become to represent. Protecting their superficial right as a private company to trounce the interests of Westerners while rigging political discourse and the market in the favor is known in some circles as 'Tactical Libertarianism', which fallaciously uses basic, unnuanced, libertarian positions to consolidate their power or to weasel their way out of an uncomfortable situation, such as defending censorship on social media. All that matters to Woke Capital is to solidify their quasi-monopolistic status by any means necessary. Woke Capital has far exceeded their capacity as simple providers of goods and services. Woke Capital has commandeered social trends: woven itself into social life, governments, the Narrative Complex. It simply cannot be viewed as a value free economic tool, providing goods and services for consumers as they now play a role in rigging the game: making consumers feel, desire, and act in a certain way which will be an economic benefit for megacorporations. Simple economic laws aren't enough to explain away this recent phenomenon. It would be disingenuous to dismiss their social overreach due to their being private companies. We're beyond that. A merely materialistic or economic analysis of megacorporations will be inadequate as they're deserving of a more philosophical appraisal. Megacorporations heavily influence both politics and lifestyle. As they have become a political force, treating Woke corporations as 'private companies', in the same category as small businesses, also being 'private companies', despite their inability to influence politics and lifestyle to their advantage, would verge on insanity. They are political entities – and should be treated accordingly. Antiquated mainstream free market theories, in large part, fail to consider the socially rearranging impact of major corporations. Not only do they spearhead shifts in social consciousness, but also push for immigration, offshoring, and other forms of deindustrialization which alter the local social composition; promoting deterritorialization, inauthenticity, and alienation.

The phenomenon of Woke Capital is an inversion of metapolitics: by promoting a cultural politicized social cause, major corporations can bring about a more consumerist society by 'coolifying' certain political ends whose metapolitics is more materialistic, vapid, and likely to separate adherents with their money for less meaningful ends. In other words, it's a form of social engineering to maximize profit margins and to forge desired political ends. In metapolitical terms: materialism, consumerism, hedonism, sexual freedom, high time preferences, and so forth, invigorated by the youthful energy of their enthusiastic young consumers and political adherents, can be conflated with left-wing politics. Right-wing politics is often viewed as sterile, mummified, and low energy, while adhering to less mainstream, uncool, traditions or customs. Woke Capital, instead of guiding lifestyles for political ends, guides political ends to bring about certain lifestyles, applying social pressures which create incentive structures for the more politically uninitiated to: 1) consume more of a particular 'woke' brand 2) support the political ends which midwife a more consumerist society 3) support political ends, and, by extension, parties who continue to protect the economic stability/status/monopoly of 'woke' corporations and 4) act as an affront to sterile, mummified, and low energy traditions.

The point has been underscored by the recent events following the George Floyd killing and consequent Black Lives Matter protests. So-called "influencers" on social media posted a black square on #blackouttuesday to connote solidarity with the protests that claimed several lives. Those who failed to do so were harried by their peers and "cancelled," which, in today's hyper social media conscious electronic age, is a fate worse than death. But it does not end there: aside from extremely social media conscious individuals out for the blood of anti-progressive heretics, corporations will axe you for failing to support psy-opped social movements. And it doesn't have to be you, specifically, at fault to elicit termination of contract or social cancellation. If a loved one makes an unwoke gesture or remark, your head can next roll off the scaffold. LA Galaxy released Serbian player Aleksander Katai after his wife made social media posts in her own language unsupportive of BLM. NASCAR racer Conor Daly had a sponsor pull out after his father said the N-words decades ago. A thirteen-year-old boy was expelled from school and his parents sacked from their jobs after a witchhunt led by a burnt out teenage celebrity after he said "guacamole n**** penis" in a social media video. And on a side note, violence against white people is being justified under unsubstantiated claims that they may have dropped a racial slur. A Flint Macy's salesman was beaten by a black customer, but it was fine because he allegedly said the N-word. Police found no proof of the assault being triggered by a racial slur, but the enraged mob didn't care – they were only out for blood. Soon enough, even if there's no proof of a racial slur before a brutal beating, the mob will justify violence by claims of "well, he was thinking it." The fact is, none of these people – NONE – are genuinely offended by these words; they are simply exercising power, nothing more. The state, every institution, major corporation, and entity caters to their caprices. What we are witnessing is a soft Reign of Terror, reinforced by neoliberalism. Think, say, do the wrong thing and your ability to provide for your family will be severely curtailed. Few are happy to live under this; they are socially conscious enough to avoid reprisal from the mob by mindlessly parroting the inane talking points and supporting the social cause for the day. Foucault, à la Bentham, imagined a 'Panopticon' where citizens had no privacy and they would be policed by each other to instill conformity. And this is what we are seeing here: you have no privacy in your opinions. The neoliberal establishment, apart from razing dissident right-wing circles on social media, does remarkably little to ensure thought policing on a societal scale. Adherents of cancel culture take care of that for them. On almost a daily basis, we witness a mass psychosis urging people to live as inauthentically as possible or else. Power will always exist, but it certainly has evolved. However, little exceeds the technocratic tyranny of today. It's almost capitalist contrived consent as your life hinges on being an active participant in the prevailing socially-accepted politics. You must have an opinion, and it has to be the correct one.

Of course, if the fear of reprisal in the form of financial restrictions and becoming persona non grata or homo sacer in a disgraceful unpersoning, to the point where you have to change name and relocate to off-grid Wyoming, doesn't frighten you, there is a secondary enforcement of progressivism in the fear of violence. Rioters will gleefully vandalize and burn small businesses – it doesn't matter to megacorporations, in fact, it's a boon as smaller competitors are taken out of the market. But threats of violence underpin unpersoning. Why do people fear doxxing? Well, it's a surrendering of one's privacy. Tucker Carlson had incensed mobs come to his home; Cassandra Fairbanks had to move state. Would it matter if a wayward crazy went to your home and attacked you. Just ask Rand Paul and his collapsed lung or the Republican baseball game that became target practice for a Bernie Bro. Their irremediable worldviews are ample justification for the kangaroo courts of the progressive banana republic. Don't forget, though, they are the oppressors. Despite every major corporation, financial institution, media outlet, sports franchise, business, influencer, et al, supporting the other team, the straight white male is still the oppressor, and America is violently racist with structural systemic racism keeping minority groups down.

In relation to the meteoric rise of 'Woke Capital', three memes have arisen in conjunction with the vibrant explosion of pro-progressive support from major corporations. Controversially, much of the affinity for progressive politics has been, on a marketing and Human Resource level, due to the rise in people who would be more receptive to a progressive message: women. Since the 1960s, the number of women in the workforce has increased tremendously. Jobs, in order to accommodate a labor supply shock with the sudden addition of university-educated women, had to be created within corporations. Marketing and Human Resources has absorbed part of that supply shock. Unmarried women, according to the data, tend to be on the left. The progressive message can infiltrate corporations with ease. Not only have corporations allied themselves with left-of-center politics, but have also become a meme to demonstrate the unaesthetic brand-laden landscape with the 'Rest Stop Nationalism' meme. A clustered rest stop/strip mall with colorful brands as a means to illustrate America's materialistic side. This meme has been met with plenty of negativity, ranging from anger, derision, to vitriol.

CHAPTER
6

JOURNALISM, ACTIVISM, and FREE SPEECH

"Journalists should be watchdogs, not lapdogs."
—Newton Lee

"Journalism is the one solitary respectable profession which honors theft (when committed in the pecuniary interest of a journal,) & admires the thief....However, these same journals combat despicable crimes quite valiantly—when committed in other quarters."
—Mark Twain

JOURNALISM IS DEAD – it is political activism writ large. Very few genuine journalists enjoy any social influence – and it is almost by design. The media has a hard time containing their resentment for non-establishment, non-globalist, political causes embodied by the rise of Western right-wing populism. Both privately and publicly run media outlets aren't subtle in concealing their partisanship. Turn on CNN or MSNBC and you'll hear them bemoan alleged Russian involvement in election meddling which saw Trump sworn into office. BBC audiences for talk shows are stacked with ideological adherents who will decry Brexit, austerity, or anything identifiably non-progressive. Despite the Mueller report being a big, fat, nothingburger – a distraction from the truth – the media won't take their foot off the pedal. They need to continue to disseminate this story. Too much has been staked on the Russia narrative. They would simply lose all credibility if a contrived 'Russian' election meddling scandal were proved to be false after having gone all in, throwing caution and integrity to the wind. And there's more than just credibility on the line. The narratives they've floated have drifted so far from truth itself, the media now has to obfuscate, misdirect, and smear in order to keep themselves relevant. Now, there's no need to ensure whether a story is true, only that it coincides with their narratives, leading to a series of I-told-you-so's by artificially inflating their chosen and questionable stories while downplaying others. For example, the media ran with a story involving high schoolers donning MAGA Hats with one smirking at a Native American elder. The media painted the high schoolers as racist, with one media pundit, Reza Aslan, tweeting the smug kid had a "more punchable face". A few months later, a black parolee was arrested for raping a random white woman. The justification given by the perp was that it was revenge for slavery. There's no evidence for the woman's ancestral participation in an abhorrent activity which was abolished by her very co-ethnics – but that doesn't matter. The story was barely touched upon because it wasn't politically profitable; the story didn't coincide with their narrative of whites – which you cannot be racist against – being a dangerous, racist, inherently evil, colonizing, destructive force. What would constitute as an authentically 'racist' crime, according to their own moral framework, isn't widely reported as it would negatively affect their narrative, thus hampering their credibility, their cultural hegemony. What's important is for the wider public to believe in their reporting and the narrative. It doesn't even need to be a huge proportion of the public: just enough to enforce narrative-inspired moral policing to quash any potential counternarratives before they gain sufficient traction to provoke political change. As the media, entertainment, Hollywood, academia, megacorporations, and pretty much every single major institution unanimously follow progressive ideals, in spite of vast swathes of the public rejecting their narratives, progressives now have to power to derail one's reputation, indirectly terminate employment, ruining future opportunities, and destroy one's life for failing to conform to the prevailing narratives. Oftentimes, the practice of publicizing one's name, address, employment, past, is called 'doxxing' (or 'doxing'). Lives have been irreparably damaged by this practice – doxxing. Unfortunately, doxxing hasn't been limited to political activist groups such as Antifa or private citizens with narrative-aligned ideological sympathies, but journalists have become embroiled in scandals where private citizens have been doxxed by active journalists. Furthermore, during the 2016 US Presidential Election, the vast majority of private journalist donations went to The Democratic Party. How is the public supposed to trust the media's reporting if there's so much, at political stake, on the line?

The way The Narrative Complex has reconstructed reality to further their revolutionary political agenda, taking society to uncharted territory, not for the betterment of mankind, but for the furtherance of their wealth and station; objective truth has to be obfuscated, misreported, or understated in order to retain credibility. Truth itself has been long abandoned by The Narrative Complex. All that matters is securing cultural influence and institutional power – by whichever means necessary. But, singing a lie loud enough, won't eventually make it truthful. The truth will eventually out. The truth will reveal itself to those who aren't sold the grandiose lies of the Narrative Complex. The narratives will become and have become so incredible that many have taken to the internet to evade the omnipresent narrativization of Pop Culture, the news, and practically every facet of contemporary living. We are currently living in a Panopticon where those who wish to express politically incorrect views must practice vigilance to ensure that somebody who may report them, isn't listening. People are self-policing their language, in many places, to avoid wrongthink being spoken in the wrong social setting. In liberal cities, confessing politically incorrect views can amount to total ostracism or worse. Multiple social pressures in the most liberal cities force narrative-aligned conformity to prevailing socially-acceptable politics. Incentive (or, more accurately, disincentive) structures are erected to remove wrongthink from the political arena, creating political enclaves on the coasts or

Democratic-dominated cities – the Clinton Archipelago. But, is it right? Doesn't matter, right is whatever the Narrative Complex's stooges tell you. You will feel a sense of accomplishment by merely agreeing with your moral and intellectual superiors with a NYT column. You'll be an intellectual too. The main issue stems from a complete lack of exposure to contradictory viewpoints from an early age: every major institution thinks a certain way – correctly. From childhood, the media, academia, entertainment, Hollywood, your teachers, everybody parrots the same politically correct vistas, and, conversely, those who think differently are knuckle-dragging unenlightened fools from Flyover Country or the Bible Belt. And instead of education, these people are utterly irretrievable, unsalvageable, beyond forgiveness. They're not worth anyone's time. They must be demographically displaced. Their values must be undermined. They have no pre-assigned role in the beautiful progressive tapestry skilfully woven by the Narrative Complex. Alienating a shrinking middle/blue collar America will, rightfully, elicit a reaction. That reaction was embodied by the election of a certain Donald J. Trump. Although Trump's presidency turned out to a little underwhelming when it came to key issues which secured his election – illegal immigration, DACA, deindustrialization, the wall – Trump's greatest service was to massively discredit the media, and, most importantly, the narrative.

Around 2015-2017, it was impossible to turn on the TV or glance through one's social media feed without being bombarded with rabidly anti-Trump articles from practically every publication. Many articles and headlines were poorly constructed, blatantly published to represent an anti-Trump narrative to filter into public consciousness to negatively depict Trump. Trump's character – and the character of his supporters – was called into question by the entire Narrative Complex. It, at one point, became nauseating. The fact that the propaganda was tirelessly peddled to an increasingly wearisome audience, despite plummeting media credibility ratings, goes to show both the short-termism (high time preferences) and political despair of the mainstream media. The mainstream media revealed itself as a propagandist, glorified political activist, and little else. This has been a great service to not only Americans – but the rest of the world. Sadly, for the media, they faltered to their own power hunger – they got caught with their hand in the cookie jar. In frenziedly attempting to derail an existential threat to their narrative, cultural, and institutional hegemony, the media, having overplayed their hand, forced millions to the alternative media. However, the shift away from the mainstream media was somewhat direct, too. Trump's anti-CNN slogans at his rallies did play a hand, by creating a meme, in shifting credibility away from the mainstream media. The unprecedented arrival of the internet – and, consequently, the decentralization and democratization of information – has changed the balance of power, the monopoly on information. Now, major corporations, Big Tech, the media, and expressly political forces have colluded to censor the flow of information online, under the banner of clamping down on 'hate speech' and 'fake news'. The internet's arrival has been nothing short of catastrophic for the powers that be; the internet's existence has been a form of anti-trust to the monopolists on information insofar as they cannot control the discourse without shutting down neo-samizdat. As everyone can access the news at the touch of a button, the nature of power has evolved considerably: it's no longer feasible to simply control the airways. Government legislation must be drafted in order to silence problematic social media users. And, when legislation isn't enough, journalists can malign alternative social media platforms such as Gab as being a "haven for white supremacists" due to the number of politically incorrect users who've been forced onto the platform after multiple suspensions. But, don't you know that X social media site is a private company and can do whatever they want?! Let the market decide! It does, indeed, get pretty difficult to simply let the market decide if the consumers comprising the market have their demands, information, and values altered by the very social media company's algorithms to alter political outcomes. Besides social media companies ramping up their censorship, honing their censorship techniques, tweaking their algorithms, etc, Trump's presidency has irreparably damaged their reputation and the reputation of mainstream journalists.

Several clickbait news sites have seen sharp falls in revenue since Trump's election. Although, this may not be totally attributable to Trump's presidency, but also a shift in public interests; there has been a decline in revenue for many media outlets across the board.

Before the election, articles urging deindustrialized Middle America to 'learn to code' were written. This particular demographic was hit particularly hard by neoliberal economics and globalist pro-immigration policies. Telling this demographic to 'learn to code' came across as insensitive, revealing the seething contempt many progressive journalists harbor for Middle America. However, when entire departments of media outlets were made redundant, tweeting 'learn to code' at certain journalists and publications at their recent loss of employment would be met with suspension from the platform. This indicates a certain power wielded by the mainstream media – even over social media to force retaliated taunts off the platform to protect the flimsy sensitivities of neurotic journos. Call them 'snowflakes' or 'weak' if you will, but, the fact remains, that these snowflakes can get you booted from social media for daring to use their own insults against them. These journalists, being propagandists and activists, for, in large part, the Democratic Party, can use their power to worse, more insidious effect, than just getting a 20-year-old dude with an anime avatar kicked off Twitter. Journalists dismissed Democratic hopeful Tulsi Gabbard's recent success following the first Democratic debate, as simply down to Russian Bots and Alt-Right trolls rigging search results and polls. Gabbard, one of the few decidedly anti-war candidates, exposed the extreme sycophancy of the establishment-brown-nosing mainstream media by pressuring them into suggesting that no sane individual would be intrigued by her more nuanced positions, deviating off the script. Most Americans wouldn't support another pointless foreign entanglement in the Middle East or wherever else. But, here's how a narrative is constructed: Tulsi, a non-establishment candidate whose positions could resonate with a lot of voters, is aligned with the 'alt-right' – a go-to media buzzword to describe the politically evil portion of the right – thus discrediting her via guilt by association. While Tulsi has gathered significant interest from some of the alt-right, due to her anti-war stance, skewing search results heavily in her favor after the debate is a little much, even for the so-called 'Russian bots' and 'alt-right'. But, that's besides the point: what matters is that she's been associated with a morally evil political faction, she's now a candidate whose views are supported by bad people. In so doing, Tulsi's views which part ways with the remainder of the Democrat establishment are viewed as wrong, implying that the opposite be linked with what might be right. By associating being anti-war with the alt-right (i.e. wrong, evil, bad) the implied inversion would mean that it's good to at least acquiesce with the pro-war position. People often wondered where the anti-war progressives went when Obama was elected in 2008 and doubled-down on Bush's foreign policy, destabilizing three countries and bombing seven.

Most recently, with the George Floyd killing, the media openly supported the Black Lives Matter protests-cum-riots and major publications even published suggestive opinion pieces about which statues to target next. The media openly lied about the so-called peaceful protesters, when dozens of cities were ablaze. The media suppressed crime data to further their narrative. When the three-month-old Ahmaud Arbery "jogger" killing during a botched citizens arrest failed to rile up sufficient anger – in the run-up to an election, no less – that story was dropped like a lead balloon and memoryholed when the Minneapolis PD knelt on the former drug dealer, porn star, and armed robber's neck for a little under nine minutes. This story was a godsend for the media. They could cart out several fallacious op-eds declaiming white privilege and continue to bash those flyover country reprobates. But, with every power structure, humiliation of the vanquished is a feature, not a bug. The quasi-canonization of George Floyd and the multiple memorials – pivoting on the coronavirus social distancing narrative – was simply another humiliation ritual. But when it came to other, non-progressive forms of assembly, then COVID-19 re-emerged as a potential threat. It was almost as if the coronavirus exclusively infected non-progressive protesters, or something.

When the George Floyd media eruption cooled, Atlanta PD shot another black man, Rayshard Brooks, dead. Needless to say, the media grossly misrepresented the shooting, and the Wendy's franchise where the shooting took place was burned to the ground. Even after clear footage showed Brooks resisting arrest, wrestling with two officers, scrap, punch, steal and fire a taser at the officers, the media attempted to re-write what people saw with their very eyes, insulting their intelligence to salvage their narrative. Following on from how the neoliberal cancel culture panopticon unpersons relatives of wrongthinkers, the stepmother of one of the officers was fired from her job for what her stepson did. The question remains: how many people would still be alive, how many businesses wouldn't have had to close their doors, and how many people's lives have been irreparably ruined through the viciously inauthetic lifestyle they were coaxed into by the media?

Many of the racial grievance grifters play the victim: they're oppressed, or claim to fight on the side of the oppressed. The reality, more often than not, is they earn a cushy 6-figure salary writing some inane column peppered with critical theory terminology, decrying the evils of systemic racism and whiteness in America. More often than not, they're invited to rub shoulders with local elites and offered a considerable platform to promote their latest book poking holes in the society which offered them unparalleled luxuries they would never have enjoyed in their home country. More often than not, they do what they do out of self-interest – don't forget, if whiteness were so bad, they wouldn't exclusively date or marry white people; which is something of a phenomenon with outspoken POC race hucksters. And who wouldn't want to be oppressed? It grants you unearned status, resources, wealth, job positions at influential mainstream publications, prestigious awards, affirmative action, the ability to fedpost about other groups who would be instabanned if they said the same thing about you. Flocks of hypersensitive people will swarm to your defense if anybody dares to criticize anything you say, no matter how inflammatory – many such cases! The media, megacorporations, financial institutions, politicians, and so on, are all on your side – being oppressed sounds awesome, I dare say.

Politics is everything. It's all that matters to journos. A significant number of media outlets wouldn't be able to stay afloat financially, retain their social media clout, or continue to influence millions who have been pre-programmed by Academia and Entertainment to support their political spin, if it weren't for unprofitable financial backing. As standalones, without the help of their backers, many would go the way of the dodo – or Gawker. But what matters is to be able to preserve a society committed to progress, keeping big business profitable and Establishment politicians in power. In a society where values aren't inextricably linked to progress and equality, many journalists wouldn't command such power or influence – which is what reinforces their support for the Establishment, prevailing socially-acceptable politics. Journalists are given an inordinate amount of influence, clout, and status in return for devotion to the cause of progress. They are able to elevate themselves to a position of power they otherwise wouldn't be afforded. Male Buzzfeed journalists measured their testosterone levels, and, despite being relatively young, had testosterone levels of elderly men. Studies have linked low-T men with having progressive views. High testosterone is linked to competitiveness – something which journalists, on the whole, shun in favor of keeping oligopolistic status: if it weren't for special interests or donors, many publications would struggle to remain profitable. Journalism is a method for low-T people – both men and women – to have impact. Presently, mainstream journalism isn't quite merit-based, rather, it is support-based. By issuing support for the Establishment, the prevailing socially-accepted politics, and the Narrative, people who would struggle on a level playing field, are endowed with the luxury to enjoy unearned impact. For the Establishment, in order to remain intact and in control of Narratives which could be considered as being detrimental to the best interests of the nation, they recruit individuals who may feel betrayed by their countries for their inability to exercise their will honorably due to their innate inadequacies. In offering an unmissable opportunity to command power and influence, loyalty to the Establishment can be almost guaranteed. No matter what insidious warmongering, politician, cover-up, or event is needed to be pushed, the Establishment lapdog journalist can be counted on. They have given up autonomy to be a part of something greater. By controlling the flow of knowledge, they can concretize their power. Additionally, when competitors emerge, threatening their monopoly on truth, instead of out-competing them, they will have the plug pulled on their ability to disseminate what is termed 'hate speech'. Media corporations and journalists pester woke capitalists into banning problematic purveyors of 'hate speech' from their platforms to hush them up. Unfortunately, this isn't a form of real market competition. Saying that X, Y, or Z is a private company, and they can do whatever they want isn't helpful. It's disingenuous to suggest this as non-market forces come into play to tilt the market – in this case, for knowledge and narratives –

in their favor. The rise of the internet broke up the cartelized outflow of information – and they don't like it. They have revealed their ugly, tyrannical, face in trying to recuperate their lost monopoly on truth. Journalists will go to extraordinary, underhanded, lengths in order to protect their cushy artificial position of power. Heaven help anybody who poses a threat to their order. Journos, hacks, quacks, and charlatans will fully employ their artificially granted position of power to reach a wide readership to smear those who threaten their industry. There is no unbiased, factual, reporting – only moral judgements made according to their fraudulent neo-secular morality which falls in line with the prevailing socially-accepted politics.

CHAPTER
7

THE BETRAYAL OF POLITICS

"Every election is a sort of advance auction sale of stolen goods."
—H.L. Mencken

"Democracy represents the disbelief in all great men and in all elite societies: everybody is everybody else's equal, 'At bottom we are all herd and mob."
—Friedrich Nietzsche

POLITICS HAS CEASED to serve the common man, but instead higher interests. Politicians can prostitute themselves and their countries to corporate power. A country can be sold out for a little status plus a few kickbacks. The Average Joe will suffer the consequences of the actions of self-serving politicians. The politician can avoid the consequences of their actions: they will either be dead by the time the consequences of their policies come to fruition, or living in a cushy gated community. Modern democracy has politicians thinking in election cycles, rather than what's best for the country. What can get them re-elected, without much regard towards the future, is all that matters. The country can go to hell –

as long as the politician who imposed destructive legislation is out of office or six feet under when the proverbial hits the fan. Who cares about the national debt, mass immigration, demographic change, ailing race relations, divorce rates, birth rates, suicide epidemics, opioid epidemics? All that matters is power, but a power whose foundations rest upon untruth. By deviating from the natural order of things, there's bound to be a self-correction of some description: the chickens must come home to roost. All of these social issues are, in the long run, unsustainable. But in the long run we're all dead – a modern nihilistic credo which left economics and has permeated wider society. A society that has lost its self-confidence, only to be subsumed by consumerist temptations, will stand idly by as politicians spout empty platitudes while acting according to their wealthy backers, to the detriment of the rest of the nation. Alternatively, the local population will endure a sustained assault attacking their heritage, history, faith, and very being rendering the concept of the nation as something not worth preserving. Meanwhile, through a combination of consumerism and critique, the host population opens itself up to the prospect of mass immigration from a divergent stock, forming a quasi-balkanized rift within that society. The new population enters and outbreeds the host population while being endowed the possibility to vote, organize politically, and consume social programs to which they've never contributed. The more socio-economically vulnerable members of the host society have been abandoned by their political representatives for a newer, more hedonistic, globalist form of politics. Those who wish to conserve the previous social order have had their principles repurposed to fit within the purview of prevailing socially-accepted politics, thus debasing their initial message, and rendering them utterly ineffectual as a realistic political force. Both sides of the aisle have thrown themselves into a neoliberal embrace which requires the nation to be offered up as a blood sacrifice to an elitist world order.

The 1960s was perhaps the most destructive decade in American history. From the Hart-Cellar Act, to multiple civil rights movements, welfare reforms, and radical social change – somewhat praised by both mainstream political factions – the political landscape also changed dramatically, to the detriment of the American electorate. The political left abandoned its stance as a force protecting the working class from deindustrialization, economic issues, social ailments, and the excesses of ascendant global capital. Today, the political left – as the undisputed cultural hegemon – now stands for critical theory, attacking anything white and American, protecting formerly marginalized social groups, promoting open borders, generous welfare, globalism, hedonism, degeneracy, sexual freedom, late-term abortions, forced income equalization, and so on. It abandoned its former base, in part, because aside from economic assistance, it had little else to offer. The 1960s saw a departure from more traditional social values in favor of unbridled, consequence-free hedonism. After the Second World War, nationalism became an unsavory political message. Nationalism clashes with the preservation of a globalist, secular, capitalist order. Corporations, with few exceptions, have embraced modern left-wing social principles to promote a more atomized and consumerist society. Power is a slippery customer, with dreadful consequences if it falls into the wrong hands. Old America has definitely felt the consequences of the need for power. Within two-party democracies, in order to gain power ad infinitum, one political side must offer something the other cannot. As mentioned, given the rise in living standards, peaking in the 1950s, the political left had to become more inventive to make themselves relevant within a political circus. Accepting a doctrine of permanent revolutions, playing off perceived inequalities, and presenting themselves as both saviors and revolutionaries, while being the political and cultural hegemons, they can position themselves to claim political power more efficiently than a low energy, stale, pale, and male pre-existing order. Aside from permanent revolution, by altering laws to change the demographics of the nation to one which tends to favor their style of redistributionist politics – at the expense of the waning host stock – they can simply change the electorate to their favor. To hell with the nation and the aging, bigoted, white working class. Could they please die quietly and hurriedly? They play no role in the future vision of the country.

Up until the Obama Administration, the mainstream left vigorously opposed foreign, Neocon-inspired, intervention. Yet as soon as Obama continued the unpopular entanglements, the mainstream left hushed their enthusiastic antiwar tone. Although the abandonment of pointless interventionism may have affected the credibility of the mainstream left from a centrist perspective, it underscores a wider problem within party politics in a secular age: the rise of cults of personality. Both political wings idolize certain statesmen and figureheads, it's only natural to do so. However, this propensity to form cults of personality seems to be more prominent among the left. The left's politics, on the whole, are vastly secular, godless. Whereas, on the right, religion tends to be given greater importance, and, therefore, a political cult of personality would clash with most religious teaching. In a sense, left-wing politics in itself has become a secular religion in a post-Christian West. With the philosophical death of God, something Nietzche was able to point out was coming way back in the 19th Century, we have witnessed a rise in the self-deification of the individual, putting their needs and whims above almost everything else. Without God in the picture, statesmen and women aren't beholden to a divine entity above themselves, and are not subject to scrutiny, in the form of eternal judgement. Additionally, as God is out of the picture in much of polite society, the bulk of individuals need some form of spiritual guidance – even in a secular form. Politics has partly filled in the void for where God once rested. A new priesthood has revealed itself in the form of celebrities, actors, media personalities, talking heads, corporations, academics – forming part of the Narrative Complex to shape your new Logos. According to a few studies, the mainstream left operates in a cult-like fashion, where people are forced to unfriend those close to them if they have "unacceptable" political views. Many behaviors suggest the modern left represents a metacult: reacting acerbically to current events, unquestioningly accepting narratives, and having a secular morality constructed around a political agenda which goes against their best interests. It may be against one's best interests, but every vaunted intellectual parrots the same identical position. And you don't want to be a dumb persona non grata, do you?

"By getting a cushy dopamine hit in unswervingly agreeing with their policies – despite their intentions – the prevailing socially-accepted politics adherent could argue for their own existence to be discarded while simultaneously believing in their own superior intelligence in the process. Almost any policy can be passed through – no matter how ludicrous – as long as agreement for said policy was associated with intelligence. If the brainiac talking heads unanimously agree with it, it must be good, right? Policies promoting high time preferences, which have become undisputable political mainstays – welfare, graduated taxation, inflation, social liberalization, sexual freedom – remain unchallenged as the vast majority of society's intelligentsia agree with them uncritically. Criticism could spell ostracism. Nobody wants to feel dumb or left out. Consent can be manufactured by demonstrating the unanimity of the most intelligent public figures in following a certain political talking point through their promotion in the media."

Sadly, many individuals married into the prevailing socially-accepted political narratives have had their lives irreparably ruined. There are incentive structures and social pressures in certain social rungs which shepherd people into unequivocally espousing left-of-center views. Some narratives promoted by the media and Entertainment depict characters living impossible lifestyles which are represented as being cool. Why get married, have children, start a family, live a quieter life, practice a religion when every 'cool' influencer does the opposite? Moreover, as previously stated, there's always a threat of the instability that accompanies social ostracism if one dares to stray away from the ideological reservation. In becoming a form of secular faith, tied to a globalist political agenda: adherents of leftist viewpoints have become reduced to pawns in furthering a political agenda for a small capitalist elite. They have, unsuspectingly, become useful idiots. However, they've been assured by the uniformity of the intellectuals elites of their righteousness – to the point where, not only will they throw their society away, they will do it with a smile on their face, basking in their superior intellect. The Narrative Complex will reward them with a warming dopamine hit for their virtuous service. But what could've been of their lives had they been not sold a lie? Could they have lived more authentically, closer to their being, if it weren't for the Narrative Complex? Almost certainly. The Narrative Complex has altered the lives of millions. Millions have been conned into believing their past is unspeakable, their civilizations based on raping and pillaging the down-trodden masses. Consequently, they've been tricked into loathing themselves for things they didn't do, based on an erroneous apprehension of their past. Social pressures dictate that, if one were to abandon this guilt or hypertolerance, they'd become a persona non grata in their social circles. The New Left, as an ideological movement in the 1960s, betrayed the Old Left – just as Neoconservatives betrayed regular conservatives. What does the left now represent? Nothing, really – except power. All it represents is whatever the Narrative Complex says is trendy. The media jumps from outrage to outrage as a means to distract, obfuscate, and misdirect. Megacorporations push socially acceptable trendy woke causes to boost sales. Left-wing politicians in lockstep with the media act without principles to corner their opponents. Any trick, no matter how dirty, must be played to secure power; after all, it's a lot easier when the Narrative Complex is on your side. Failing that, they can always project or call their opponent a racist. And this is why the left wins: they hold their enemies accountable to their principles while having none themselves. Those with principles are quickly weeded out as being unsuitable for the grand scheme of progress. Principles are nothing more than a stumbling block to those after unlimited power, while trying to pass off a friendly facade in a democratic arena.

A blind eye has been turned to the left's recent unholy marriage to megacorporations. Left-wing capitalism – neoliberalism, globalism, Woke Capital – has almost become an unspoken mainstay to the mainstream left – all because the bulk of megacorporations unabashedly support their viewpoints and candidates. Their sins of filthy profiteering, privatization, and inequality can be forgiven due to their cultural placement. Gone are the days where left-wing establishment politicians vocally denounce the excesses of the 'free market'. Now, many of the regulations passed under left-wing causes in fact benefit the megacorporations they seek to tame. Regulations imposed for environmental reasons – often associated with left-of-center politics – squeeze the competition for megacorporations. Although protecting the environment is a good cause, many policies end up having negative economic consequences. As megacorporations exercise the power to change culture through consumerism, then social media, they have been the greatest driving force in shifting the Overton Window to the left. With a relatively 'free' market, given that individuals are innately unequal, wildly disparate results will occur. Despite the general left wing point of departure being: 1) a move towards equality and 2) maximum social freedom – embracing a socially liberal form of capitalism will promote more inequality as part of a Faustian deal. Economic and social equality will slowly become more untenable given the cultural shift of megacorporations towards the left. Then, when economic inequality rises again, social freedom will have to diminish in order to address the rising inequality. Presently, the mainstream left stands for a capitalist and socialist synthesis which has shifted from the two post-Enlightenment modern forces: liberalism and communism. Liberalism's ontology isn't grounded in any identifiable fixed destination – except for the preservation of property, which, in part, it has failed to do. Liberalism has shapeshifted into progressivism which shamelessly employs capitalism as its economic and social engine room to propel the all-encompassing polito-cultural leviathan. Leftism, since the Civil Rights Era, has backslid away from protecting the predominantly white working classes to circling around minorities, LGBT, and unfettered social liberalization to create the most atomization, thus nihilism, eliciting a demand for greater state presence to mitigate greater levels of chaos and conflict, and, from a philosophical view, to fill in the void as a secular religion in the absence of one dominant religion. The departure away from Marxist Class Theory has been predictable in a globalist techno-capitalist economy: now, we are treated to intersectionality which plays upon pre-existing concepts of Class struggle. Anybody, who so identifies, can become a part of any intersection. Class Theory has been broadened to include anybody – except cis, heterosexual, white males. In political terms, this is wonderful when pretending to act within the relatively rigid parameters of two-party democratic politics. How can you win over and over and over again? Simple – you rig the game. You introduce new moral frameworks which benefit your political ends. You demonize those who refuse to conform to your new moral framework. You import millions of new, hyper-fertile voters, who will statistically vote for you in exchange for plenteous social welfare at the expense of the host stock. You ally yourself with megacorporations and have the Narrative Complex's backing to create false consumer demand and commandeer a monopoly on truth. Power is all that matters. Those who used to be your main voting base aren't reliable. In fact, they've got to go. They won't become part of the beautiful unprecedented social experiment, us, as moral and intellectual superiors, have concocted for you.

On the right, although demographically speaking, the Republican party seems to be the party of White America, for now. However, many mainstream personalities have spouted views, principles, and ideas antithetical to the aforesaid demographic. "America is ideas" is one of the pilloried platitudes from the mainstream right, which is, in fact, consistent with some classical liberal principles upon which it was founded, but reflects a form of nihilism birthed out of the 1960s idealism which some older conservatives still espouse. Over the past 50 years, the media-friendly mainstream right has taken it upon themselves to become as unelectable and unpalatable as they possibly can to an electorate increasingly beholden to social norms constructed by media narratives. Former Trotskyites formed the Neoconservative movement which hijacked the right's patriotism for endless foreign intervention towards a Trotskyite end: global revolution, in this case through forced democratization of resource-rich countries. Moreover, the right stands for 'limited government', a term upon which there is no unified definition – it is almost nebulous by design. Limited government can be expanded to support neoliberal economics which undermine every conservative value. Conservatism has been redefined to become a despised political force in the view of mainstream narratives, yet they still back policies which will simply worsen the cultural rot they pretend to rally against. By adding qualifiers to their statements on immigration, such as, "as long as they're here

LEGALLY" or utilizing a form of careless nihilism –
"I don't care what you do in the privacy of your own
home" – while, culturally, more land is ceded to the
left; not only have they devolved into being a
toothless force, but a hated one, while desperately
scrambling for headpats from the left or attempting to
expose how 'racist' they are. In the process of
pointing out the moral bankruptcy or ideological
inconsistencies of the mainstream cultural left, they
are relegating themselves to playing by standards
which are created, often capriciously, by the
Narrative Complex. They are out of their depth – and
destined to fail. The right isn't the left. Although an
obvious statement, the kind of person who may hold
right-wing beliefs probably won't want to or find the
time to organize protests, back minority causes,
promote rapid social change – be that demographic or
cultural – and a whole slew of other ontologically
non-right-wing positions. Unfortunately, for the
mainstream, they've succumbed to the liberal
paradigm – one which places rationalism above
emotion. In a democracy with universal suffrage, it is
verging on insanity to believe that the bulk of voters
guide themselves rationally over tribal or emotional
reasons. This is part of the reason why Trump
enjoyed such startling success among a more
disenfranchised White America; it wasn't entirely for
rational reasons as to why he won, but emotional
ones. A betrayed Rustbelt electorate saw their
industries relocate overseas, and watched their
neighborhoods change before their very eyes, with
nihilism and substance abuse running rampant. It's
no surprise they backed the radical candidate who

promised serious change. All in all, Trump unleashed energy with his smart 'Make America Great Again' slogan, implying that America had somehow lost its greatness, triggering a romantic wish to return to a bygone era which Americans have been denied. This populist movement, which has been sweeping its way across Europe, has sourced its energy from the disgust generated by the consequences of Globalist politics – one which has left Americans behind. In spite of incessant Narrative Complex propaganda ushering in 'white guilt', enough anger, coupled with Trump's devastatingly simple pro-America rhetoric, saw Trump's election into the White House. Trump's opposition, Hillary Clinton, simply couldn't rely on the energy mustered by her notably feminine and less white voter base – how can pro-establishment neoliberalism backed by the Narrative Complex inspire voters on a large scale? Yes, she *did* have the popular vote, but Trump won where it mattered. Since Trump's election, several articles from left-wing publications argued for the abolition of the Electoral College – for no other reason except to facilitate a Democratic Party one-party system. In the UK, hereditary peerage for the House of Lords was scrapped in 1999. The right appears to do everything in its power to ensure failure, from espousing wildly unpopular positions – almost by design – to failing to tilt the political system to their favor. Instead of taking plays out of the left's handbook, they pontificate to deaf ears about how wonderfully principled they are. In fact, you could imagine a geriatric conservative sermonizing you while toiling away in a gulag on how at least they stuck to their principles. They disarm themselves with paltry, reactive, yet spineless, politics. The Gadsden Flag's famous "Don't Tread on Me" is a defensive, reactive, form of politics. By always being on the defensive, relying on antiquated principles, and attempting to seek groveling approbation from the left, they are bound to lose every single political conflict. Recent history is a testament to their abject track record. What have conservatives actually conserved? Ronald Reagan isn't coming back, and Trump has failed to deliver his most important promises: on immigration. But it's okay – look at the GDP, the DOW has hit record highs! Fixating on materialist policies will bring about materialist ends. These are the ends they deserve. Under what has been satirized as a Gung Ho right-wing nation over the past 60 years, America has become one giant atomized multicultural strip mall. Meaning has been hollowed out and the grifters who occupy the mainstream right insist on America being merely an idea. The idea of a limited government being at the forefront of the mainstream right's mission statement is unutterably disastrous. 1913 was the final year you'd ever have a shot of coming back to a limited government. In the past fifty years, the population has more than doubled and the white voting base is soon-to-be less than 50%. How, assuming a small government politician ever gets elected again, will you go about limiting the size of the federal government to the size it was over four generations ago? America is a radically different country in many states. The federal government has grown like a malignant tumor – even under the presidency of so-called "conservatives". You don't have a chance in hell, unless the messaging changes. But there is an opportunity to exploit.

At least they stuck to their principles. That's all that really matters. Let's continually point out the moral foibles of the left – that'll work, this time. Unfortunately, for the right, it seems as if there is an innate will-to-be-left-alone. The problem is, their political adversaries rely on never taking their foot off the gas, despite the rapidly approaching brick wall at the end of the street. The mainstream right has the choice to forcefully take control of the wheel, but refuses to do so under a shroud of flimsy reasoning. The mainstream right rests on their laurels. The reactionary nature of the right disables them from taking action in preserving a social order. The failure of a class-conscious revolution in Western Europe – where capitalism was most advanced – meant that the left had to become craftier in order to create their desired social order. Drunk off post-War nostalgia and credit-fueled economic boom, the right failed to perceive their slow boiling, like the old frog's pacified metabolism in the pot. Today, the water is reaching boiling point, but a lid is being placed over the top of the cooking pot. One of the problems with the Mainstream Right is their commitment to liberalism in the form of a defense of free-market economics and raising property to a highest value: as a result, tradition, spirituality, nationhood, collective self-confidence have faltered to near extinction, with the exception of demonized esoteric pockets of the internet in the face of atomistic individualism promoted by every single quasi-establishment organization.

ANTI-WHITENESS

"What 'multiculturalism' boils down to is that you can praise any culture in the world except Western culture—and you cannot blame any culture in the world except Western culture."

—Thomas Sowell

AMERICA IS A MELTING POT – or so we're told. However, there are some who don't seem to fit into the colorful mosaic of American demographics. From around 2012, there was an astronomical rise in the number of openly, avowedly, anti-white articles pumped out by the mainstream media. The levels of gaslighting propaganda would make Edward Bernays proud. Many articles openly attack whites for past wrongs, for not voting a certain way, for the way they act; but, at the same time, race is a social construct. Of course, it ceases to be that the second it becomes politically profitable to chastise whites as a group for X, Y, or Z reason in relation to a prevailing social narrative As the media condemns White America, they often point to 'institutionalized' or 'systemic' racism – at the hands of whites – wherever a certain group fails or is overrepresented in some undesirable field such as violent crime.

Barack Obama's presidency marked the apotheosis of a post-racial America. After being ridden with strife and conflict for the succeeding two generations after the Civil Rights Era, America finally managed to overcome its racially fractious past by electing a black man as president. Racism was surely defeated – for good this time. Unfortunately, this couldn't be further from the truth. In such an expansive and populous country, with multiple diverse divergent groups, unifying them all within a two-party political state isn't exactly a fait accompli. Since 1965, the Republican Party has implicitly become the party of 'white America' judging by voting statistics and The Democratic Party's violent rupture with associating itself with a pre-1965 – white – America.

Some will venture to suggest that there exists a complex hegemonic web of white supremacy within government which must be dismantled. Alternatively, others make the case of there being white structures in place which explain radically disparate results in economic prosperity among groups. Yet, at the same time, the very same white supremacist white hegemonic superstructure which oppresses everybody meekly allows for the billion-dollar-backed mainstream media to run with daily anti-white narratives bashing white people every single day. A quick unbiased glance at data, while suppressing any a priori urges to regurgitate half-baked environmentalist demographic theories, would answer for several disparities. In other words, it's not racism or white people who are the problem – it's the Narrative Complex, special interests, and a fraudulent two-party democratic system: one party which relies on a growing non-white voter base and the other which insouciantly ignores their shrinking voter base yet vaingloriously attempts to court those who will statistically never vote for them. Of course, both groups are beholden to greater financial powers. As is the nature of modern hypercapitalist liberal democracy: everything is commodified, everything has a price – even your nation.

Some people are nostalgic to return to a time pre-Hart-Cellar, others wish for America to continue it's post-white direction full speed ahead. America has become very divided in many respects. On the one hand, the mainstream right will impotently prove to their culturally-dominant political counterparts, while tacitly yearning for a return to a more unified America; on the other, the white right will be dismissed as being inherently incorrigible for their vistas and indelible sins of whiteness – they are the Narrative Complex's boogeymen, they are to blame for all of society's ills. But, of course, although the left, as an identifiable politico-cultural entity, has been dominantly on the ascendancy since the Second World War; claims that racism has worsened in recent year, either utterly disingenuous or lacking in self-awareness to realize that their undisputed politico-cultural power has led to the current situation which they decry. Of course, the solution to these social ills is more leftist or progressive policies, including increasing immigration – which has provoked much alienation, disaffection, and atomization – especially in areas their pre-Hart-Cellar constituents lived. The mainstream right will often comically call out those evil DemoKKKrats whenever there is a riot, violent crime, or murder in one of the following cities: Detroit, Chicago, Baltimore, Washington, St. Louis, New Orleans. Of course, a problem is recognized, but, perhaps out of fear or politeness cannot name the elephant in the room. Even if there are no whites directly involved in a tragic act involving minority groups, the Narrative Complex will find a means by which to spin the story to attack whiteness or simply ignore it altogether. For example, some stories can be explained through disaffection caused by a lack of direct social welfare, which is a product of the institutional racism propped up by hegemonic whiteness, apparently. Whatever anti-white excuse is offered, the end product is an increasingly disenfranchised shrinking white majority. Once whites cease to be a numerical minority will the daily bashing end? No, hell no. After years of scapegoating whites as a bugaboo, they won't swivel on their narrative. Many articles and verified voices on social media call for the total destruction of whiteness.

CHAPTER
9

WHAT SUPPORTING TRUMP SYMBOLIZES ACCORDING TO THE MAINSTREAM

*"In half a lifetime, many Americans have seen their
God dethroned, their heroes defiled, their culture
polluted, their values assaulted, their country
invaded, and themselves demonized as extremists
and bigots for holding on to beliefs Americans have
held for generations."*
—Pat Buchanan

*"This struggle to preserve the old creeds, cultures,
and countries of the West is the new divide between
Left and Right; this struggle will define what it
means to be a conservative. This is the cause of the
twenty-first century and the agenda of
conservatism for the remainder of our lives."*
—Pat Buchanan

WHAT DOES IT MEAN to be a Trump supporter? Well, it means two things. First, the vote for Trump was a vote against the traditional two-party left-right paradigm; it was a vote repudiating globalism, mass immigration, and neoliberal economics; it was a vote against unpopular neoconservative hawkishness; it was a vote against the so-called 'Deep State.' Of course, the blue checkmark class and Narrative Complex were up in arms at Trump's election, doubling down on their anti-whiteness and every tactic which lost them their monopoly on truth and power. Calling everybody who wasn't a devout progressive or non-white a racist didn't seem to work against the wider population. Despite the failure to shame 2016 Trump supporters by hysterically calling them racist, prominent groups representing a dying mainstream conservatism took it upon themselves to bastardize and multiculturize the Trump movement by trying to prove to progressives that they are, indeed, not racist. Focus has been taken away from Trump's initial voting base and applied to groups who are least likely to vote for him. And, again, economics is invoked to prove the MAGA message's anti-racism: look at how well X group is performing! Look at those sweet unemployment figures! This leads us to the second meaning, and a newer meaning of what the Trump movement represents: a dying liberal mainstream conservatism, employing progressive tactics to silence dissidents, trying to out-progress progressives. The movement's representatives have to become gayer, blacker, trannier, and more tolerant than whatever the Democrats can muster – take that, leftists! We're better than you at being you! We can beat you at your own game, that you created, with the rules you change daily on a dime! The MAGA movement carts out all sorts of personages who wouldn't traditionally represent conservatism, which signifies Conservatism Inc's total break from real conservative values. New conservative values represent a corporate libertarianism, a belief in the immortality of the Constitution, and passivity toward demographic change, as America is only a placeholder for ideas – not a homeland.

Trump's election, in some ways, represented a last gasp of the shrinking white majority before Democrats secure a permanent demographic-democratic voting majority. The vote was a vote against the treacherous elite class who sold out the pre-1965 America. The puppet class of globalist politicians, representing the system propped up by a sophisticated concatenation of self-interest and high time preferences, was promised to be ousted. However, their redoubtable economic position transcends simple democratic politics. Politicians represent them instead of the electorate. The electorate is bovine, taxed as livestock and milked for economic productivity. Freedom means different things to different people, but has freedom increased in the last fifty years? Hardly. People have become more enslaved than ever: to their passions, consumerism, sexual urges, regulations, dependency on technology, choice – they don't have the freedom to become who they are.

CHAPTER
10

OK BOOMER AND MEME ARCHETYPES

*"And I apologize to all of you who are the same age
as my grandchildren. And many of you reading this
are the same age as my grandchildren. They, like
you, are being royally shafted and lied to by our
Baby Boomer corporations and government."*
—Kurt Vonnegut Jr.

THE OKAY BOOMER MEME has risen to prominence
pitting Zoomers and Millennials against the Baby
Boomer or those who are spiritually Boomer-esque,
regardless of their age group. The Boomer
characterizes itself through an inflated sense of
entitlement, sneering at those who weren't afforded
the opportunity to be as well-off given the radical
difference in socioeconomic circumstances. The
Boomer is a slow learner when it comes to
technology, often relying on their impatient younger
family members to periodically instruct them on how
to properly operate a smartphone. The Boomer often
ridicules himself through dogmatic devotion to
antiquated political views, comparing everything –
even soft liberalism – to Hitlerism in cringeworthy
and easily-parodied internet meme. "Okay Boomer"

in itself has become something of a pejorative. The lack of respect inherent within the short phrase condescends to The Boomer or anybody locked into the blue-pilled Boomer mindset. Saying Okay Boomer to somebody who presents an elitist, insensitive, arrogant, or unpopular point of view is akin to another pejorative: "Blue Checkmark."

Perhaps the strangest phenomenom of the 'Okay Boomer' pejorative is that it has managed to bridge political opinion. Political outsiders of both the left and right fire invective at tedious Boomers. Both the left and right nurse resentment towards what The Boomer represents, metapolitically. To the left, the dying boomer voting base is the final redoubt to a eurocentric white Western world. The Boomer represents a stifling of progress, racism, imperialism, jingoism, sexism, and an inability to connect with younger, more vibrant, generations. To the right, The Boomer stubbornly conforms to a historical revisionist view of the past set in motion by progressive academics. The Boomer is change-averse – even to their disproven views on immigration and the so-called 'Natural Conservative' fallacy. The Boomer conservative embodies a fundamentally losing political strategy for the right, lionizing destructive politicians such as Ronald Reagan, while finding refuge in their overvalued principles and an exhausted, alienable, Constitution. The Boomer political axiom is simple: the more the government does, the socialister it is. It draws on libertarian axioms, while completely ignoring any conceptions on the nature of power, the preservation of power, and tantalizing a discerning electorate.

Moreover, the point of contention which unites both dissident political wings is The Boomer's predilection for neoconservative hawkish policies to the detriment of the American people. By being the policeman of the world, the honest dissident left railed against the final throes of US imperialism and meaningless loss of life; while the right decried the endless spending, destabilization of the Middle East – which led to The (contrived) Migrant Crisis – and a delegitimization of American patriotism, often conflated with jingoistic neoconservativism and mass surveillance.

Another gripe against the Boomer critiques the generations's aggregate high time preference, leading to a slew of insolvent social programs. Under the guise of expanding the workforce in order to pay for the generous social programs, unscrupulous groups – from the mainstream left and right – lobbied to import an underclass of cheap labor from around the world. People needed cheap gardeners, pool cleaners, and maids. A few years later, California went irreversibly Blue. Texas is on course to follow suit. America's face has been all but irreversibly changed. So-called conservatives even welcome the demographic shift of America, despite voting trends spelling political suicide in a demographic-democratic arena. From an anti-capitalist perspective, the unprecedented social revolutions of the 1960s also played into the hands of megacorporations. As I mentioned in my chapter on Woke Capital, the cultural shift away from the nuclear family practically doubled the workforce, creating a quandary for the anticapitalist left: women's liberation or depressing wage rates for megacorporations. Two complaints from both political factions form an unlikely anti-boomerist alliance – something quite remarkable. The brand of liberalism championed by boomers, as a group, has been fundamentally rejected by all. Rejection isn't something that is taken kindly by the boomer generation. Some boomers go as far as to flex and dab on the younger generation's financial misfortunes, picking apart their lack of responsibility, if they dare to invoke fiscal and monetary missteps brought about by their elders' voting habits or the lifestyle choices of their youth. The right would attack the lack of self-discipline within several social revolutions which took place in the 1960s; the left would complain that boomers failed to cleanse themselves of their various -isms.

Despite valid criticisms, the Boomer meme is something of a boogeyman, a scapegoat. Most people need to apportion blame onto entities outside of their control for comfort's sake. The Boomer has entered the fray as an identifier for a boogeyman, transcending class, religious, and political lines in a world saturated by narratives. Some of the criticisms volleyed at Boomers as a whole are unfounded. But, there's plenty of righteous indignation to be fired at the Boomer. Another core theme surrounding the Boomer as a whole is what it represents: whiteness. Nobody ever imagines a Boomer as being anything other than an aged white person; somebody financially well-to-do, disconnected, pettily arrogant, but above all: white.

Although anti-Boomer sentiment isn't as prominent in the mainstream right – largely because the mainstream right endorses the 'Boomer' style of conservatism – the dissident right, although far more overtly nationalistic, identifies and critiques the Boomer generation as an exclusively white phenomenon. The dissident right detonates much of the unintentionally anti-white foundations laid by the Boomer generation, while blasting much of the Boomer's inability to leave their bastardized principles which have caused much of the havoc the dissident right condemns. The left – both mainstream and fringe – endorses some form of anti-whiteness. It is, therefore, less taboo to call out or identify the white element of the Boomer generation for those on the left. All sides of the debate, except Boomers, are to some degree aware of a racial component in the demographic-democratic political arena. If the left had lower aggregate time preferences, gloating about a non-white, progressive, America on a mass scale could have been avoided. The fact remains: they couldn't help themselves and Trump was elected. Perhaps Trump wasn't able to fulfill most of his important campaign promises on preventing a major demographic shift in the future during his first term, but most current Anti-Boomer sentiment from the right surrounds the Trumpian cult of personality social media Boomers have created.

Another reason for the left-right anti-Boomer coalition is the historical significance of the Boomer generation as a marketing group. I must stress that Boomers have been apportioned most of the blame for various social ills by the entire political spectrum. However, the age-group as a whole wasn't entirely responsible. Much of what is described to be Boomer is a mindset prevalent among older white adults.

Perhaps a reason younger generations feel betrayed by the Boomer generation is a disconnection to their past. At a time when people feel increasingly atomized, where does one turn for meaning if they can't turn to their past? Long gone is the kick-ass legacy the Boomer's parents passed down of defeating the Nazis and becoming a sickly superpower. What connects younger generations to what they are? Nothing.

Current generations live at a time where historic, received, identities are frowned upon. These identities are smeared as nativist, racist, reactionary, xenophobic and must be tossed aside to accommodate a multicultural future. Moreover, efforts to assign an identity on oneself, which will invariably become projected into demographic-democratic politics, are dismissed as 'Identity Politics.' This catch-all phrase can be used to describe – and condemn – both the political left and right. The fringe left seeks identity through intersections – sexuality, race, gender, ethnicity, ability, etc – whereas the right seeks something more primordial, nativist, and metaphysical. Both are a cause for concern to the liberal, be they left or right wing, as any self-discovery towards an identity would tend towards the dismantling of a liberal regime. For there to be any lasting semblance of a liberal democracy, a certain metaphysical oneness of the electorate must exist, be it religious or ethnic bound by mythology. America is a multicultural and pluralistic society. If all – and this also applies to multicultural liberal European democracies – members of the electorate were to adhere to the main democratic structure, regardless of their own received identity, while denying the existence of their own identities, then why do constituencies with large migrant populations vote in a representative of their own extraction? Surely it wouldn't matter who was elected.

But, returning to The Boomer, the Boomer was patient zero of a mass marketing, mass media-driven globalist economism. To fully condemn them wouldn't be fair – they didn't know any better. In light of the Boomer's unwitting cosmopolitanism, they became a missing link between the younger generations and their past, which consequently denied them a firm grounding in their identity, leaving the younger generations deracinated. This is, perhaps, why we have witnessed the secular construction of identity around so-called intersections, rather than something more self-evident such as nation or faith.

Another feature brought to the fore by unraveling current events has been the energizing of non-white identities. While we can launch lengthy invective at the toothlessness of those who oppose so-called identity politics; little is done to de-energize the unshakable identities of non-white Americans. Third generation Mexicans can wave their flags at will, black people can tirelessly promote their history, the LGBT community is endlessly celebrated by megacorporations. Okay, so what if I'm proud of being a straight white male? The left will call you every single epithet under the sun and the anti-identitarian middle ground will urge you not to succumb to identity politics. Of course, the anti-identitarians wither like a June daffodil to any other groups. While, on paper, it's a nice idea to yield one's identity for the bigger picture, all other identities have become emboldened by the Narrative Complex. There's every incentive structure in place to reinforce your identity at every turn – if you're not a straight white male, that is. The Narrative Complex actively engages in propaganda to propel non-white events and holidays, such as Kwanzaa and Juneteenth (both of which are completely astroturfed celebrations), while downplaying Christmas, defecating on Christianity from a great height. Santa Claus is now very gay, he's in an interracial gay relationship. Rudolf the Red Nosed Reindeer is also gay. Jesus was a transgender socialist. Mary wasn't a virgin. And, most importantly, you must say "Happy Holidays" over the Christmas period, otherwise you'd be excluding minorities.

As an outsider, the image of Americanism projected by Boomer Americans is something astroturfed, inauthentic, and commodified. Cool, shooting guns, a firm appreciation for private property and personal freedom is all fine and dandy, but, what then? What comes after that? The Narrative Complex has thoroughly satirized the meaning of what it is to be American to an international audience to the point where it, to many, seems to be an identity not worth preserving. Following the various neoconservative-inspired entanglements across the world, started by people elected by Boomers, America hasn't forged many unshakable friendships. Factions of the left seek a redefinition of Americanism through demographic means; in part, to secure elections via a demographic majority, and also to dilute the impact of whiteness and its uncoolness vis-a-vis a more diverse, vibrant, and energetic youth peddled by the Narrative Complex. The dissident right seeks to redefine Americanism by invigorating it with European grandeur, culture, while conjuring up a form of pre-eminence. The Boomer conservative or mainstream conservative merely seeks to maintain the Narrative Complex's representation of Americanism – guns, titties, Bud Light, flag-waving, jingoism, barbecues, and lawnmowers. Frankly, the Narrative Complex's representation offers a demeaningly materialistic image of American identity – one which troublesome Zoomers wish to completely destroy. It is an insult to reduce one's identity to saleable goods. There is more to life than just goods or services. Sadly, in a secular, narrative-saturated, online world, when one's intersections don't quite cut it, the brands one conspicuously consumes become a de facto identity in the absence of something more eternal. One's past defines one's present. History and identity are inextricably linked. People aren't destined to have self-ascribed identities plucked out of the relativist narrative-driven ether. Part of the erasure of histories – apart from the ability to recode identities within a narrow progressive paradigm – is to bury the more problematic areas of the past. But this is only for those warmly welcomed by the progressive establishment. If you said the N-word or homophobic F-word as a nobody with 19 followers as a teenager eight years ago, this is grounds for cancellation and ruining your life. But if you're a progressive icon, the past is in the past. What does it matter that somebody like George Floyd held a gun to a pregnant woman? That was in the past! Remove the past, remove the sins. This outlook on life spells trouble for most. It would not be prudent for an employer to overlook the fact that an interviewee was fired from all their past jobs for stealing on the job and missing work days without good reason. Likewise, a man looking for a loyal wife wouldn't choose the party girl with a body count higher than the Chinese kid who speaks no English on the Call of Duty server. While people make mistakes, one would be mad to forgo looking at one's past before interacting with them – and the same applies with mass immigration.

Before delving into internet meme archetypes, it must be said that memes have a shelf life. Of course, these shelf lives are unpredictable which is why some of the memes listed below might be out of date:

Bugmen/Soyboys:

WEAK METAPOLITICALLY LEFT-WING MEN who promote liberal politics to give themselves purpose. Often residing in big cities, working faceless corporate jobs or small time blogging. Despite their lack of masculinity, they gallantly bash masculinity to seek approval of women out of their league. They use social media to pander to a fraudulently overconfidence sense of vanity derived from their pitifully low natural testosterone levels. Bugmen can differ from soyboys as this could refer to a "bug-chaser" – something else entirely. Soyboys have been known to post pictures of themselves, posing with a slack-jawed grin, covering most of the focal object in the shot, and sometimes with a bottle of their favorite Soylent product.

Blue Checkmark:

A BLUE CHECKMARK is the pejorative term to describe a verified personality on Twitter. The Blue Checkmark usually has something to do with journalism or blogging, and, more often than not, espouses some form of elitist view. Many Blue Checkmarks are unknown for what it is they do. Some espouse virulently anti-white social justice positions, often drawing contempt from social media users for their woke takes, garnering frequent ratios. Their views, more often than not, are excoriated. Memes involving the cancerous views of some Blue Checkmarks have been often satirized.

The AWFL or AWFUL:

THE AFFLUENT WHITE FEMALE LIBERAL or Affluent White Female Urban Liberal is pretty much self-explanatory. The AWFL makes every effort to speak for the voiceless colored masses. She simultaneously derives social clout and self-gratification for her ethnomasochistic vistas. She brazenly speaks for others, yearning to feel oppression she believes her inferiors suffer. Often, the AWFL forgoes motherhood, diverting her motherly energies towards people of color. The AWFL is a vanguard liberal, concocting anti-Trump rants expressing her contempt toward flyover country in cabernet-sauvignon-inspired late night rants to her 8,000 Twitter followers with blue wave emojis in the Twitter bios.

Blue Wave Resister:

THIS TWITTER PERSONALITY is often a washed up Hillary supporter who still believes she was actually the winner from securing the popular vote. Sharing articles from publications calling for an abolition of the electoral college is one of the many copes exhibited by this personality. Like old boomer conservatives, the blue wave resister is intractable in their views and their memeing ability is perhaps worse. Many embrace alternative lifestyles and sexualities – their philosophy can be distilled to a deferral of consequence. Many are hippyish, never fully growing up. Many are also childless – like the AWFL – which resonates within their superficial worldview. Some seek solace in phony intellectualism by regurgitating statistics eked out by East coast brainiacs. Trump's Twitter comments are always filled by disgruntled resisters telling him to resign or posting dreadful memes under his tweets, regardless of the content. Trump could announce that he single handedly cured cancer, and he would still be called Cheeto Hitler or Orange Mussolini by his detractors.

Boomer/Normiecon:

THIS PERSONALITY IS a slowly dying breed. Normiecons, when embarking on further political self-study abandon their mainstream conservative views in favor of something harder or social-democratic/democratic socialist/soft forms of anarchism. The Boomer, however, just like the Resister, is intractable in his views. A cult of personality has been erected around Donald Trump as president, plus an over-Americanization of their content to satirical levels. In fact, the patriotic overkill is a little bit of a turn-off, likened to the cheap outsider's view of American pride. Their tweets are cringeworthy, more often than not, laden with superfluous hashtags, and small esotericisms referring to QAnon and other boomer-tier content. Many overindulge in American Eagle, lion, or Trumpian iconography, saturating their profiles with support for Trump. Many can't get enough of all the winning, defeating foreign enemies and bolstering the economy. However, celebrations may be a little premature. And, after Trump leaves office, then what? When the Trumpian golden age is over, what will happen? Will an amply swamp-draining billionaire take his place? Or will demographic shifts spell the end of the Republican party? Stay tuned.

Groypers:

THE GROYPERS ARE cheeky, young, mischievous, energetic, embodiments of the cozy toad meme. Ready to disrupt many a Q&A segment with difficult questions, the Groyper posed a counter-iteration to mainstream conservatism which is provably inauthentic, fake, and g**. They have often presented themselves, not as competitors vying to attract disaffected conservatives over to their cause, but to shatter the illusion of mainstream conservatism serving the interests of Americans, but Big Business. Politicking is rather unriveting, ossified, economized by mainstream conservatism obsessed with economics. What's offered in its stead is something less observable than numbers on a graph, but a new America, hardened by youthful energy, wronged by globalist interests, hollowed out to represented a revolving door of capital and labor in a continental strip mall. The Groypers cannot stand to live in this future the Boomers have provided them, and are angrily fighting back.

Coomer:

THIS IS, PERHAPS, a less relevant internet meme to mock those with severe porn addictions and resultant brain damage from overfapping. The coom brain ties in with the simp whose entire raison d'etre is based around chasing tail, although both employ differing modus operandi. The Coomer, worn out by several rounds of masturbation, proudly promotes the harmlessness of recreational pornography as a means to destress, take the edge off. However, his lifestyle has left him utterly unfit to pursue healthy interactions with the opposite sex and others.

Consoomer:

THE CONSOOMER CAN be personified by almost anyone. In spite of this, the consoomer often assumes the form of a soyboy or bugman whose life is defined and identity is ascribed by the brands he consumes. Meaning is given to him by consumer goods, plastering over the void in his life, staving off boredom until creative destruction takes its toll – and it's time to consume new product. Politically, the consoomer is mostly on the left – left-liberal, to be precise – but consoomers can be anywhere on the political spectrum. The majority of consoomers are atheistic. Consooming is a means to an end. They may think that living a Godless life can bring them meaning, but they never wonder what their purpose is without their consumer goods...

Doomer:

THIS POOR SOUL has swallowed and plugged the blackpill. Barely able to find purpose, the doomer struggles on pallidly saving face to be something of a part of modern society. The doomer's philosophy is an inversion of the phrase "every cloud has a silver lining" – as every silver lining has its cloud. Steeped in pessimism, the doomer's personal philosophy somewhat takes on a contemporary form of Schopenhauer's thinking. They weren't asked to be born, especially not at a time like this.

Bloomer:

A BLOOMER IS the reverse of a doomer. A thoroughgoing optimist. He has transcended the need for pessimism and finds comfort in the fatalistic nature of life. To the bloomer, everything is gonna be alright. You can imagine Bob Marley's "Don't Worry" playing on a loop as the Bloomer's theme tune, accompanying him wherever he goes. His optimism may, at times, cost him friends, but he isn't concerned; he is damn sure the future will be bright, now matter how dark it may be now.

Zoomer:

THIS GROUP IS thrown in because it rhymes with a few of the above groups. The Zoomer is a portmanteau of Generation Z and Baby Boomer. Millennials are something of a lost generation when it comes to politics. Although they tend to be a sturdy left-of-center voting bloc, Millennials, on the whole, are too preoccupied by abject credit ratings, finances, and finding an identity. Zoomers, on the other hand, have more fire in their bellies, aware of the mendacity of the Narrative Complex, to some degree. Despite some negative statistics illustrating societal decline in the form of teenage pregnancy, sexual activity, and drug use, Zoomers appear to reject much of the lifestyles lived by many Millennials. On social media, Zoomers who are politically active find appeasing fence-sitting views less attractive. Their youthful energy and memecraft will make for some very interesting scenes in the future.

Chad vs Virgin:

THE CHAD VS VIRGIN meme symbolizes the rift between a traditionally brawny, muscular "Chad" and dweebier, skinny, under-confident "Virgin." Many internet memes assume archetype as proxies for real life sentiments and interactions. Seeing as the meme has been used to display the preferences of various subcultures, fandoms, and pockets of the internet, the pre-eminence of a strong man vs his beta counterpart is almost universally recognizable, despite the Narrative Complex's best efforts to delegitimize traditional representations of true masculinity. Don't forget, a feminized society is a pacified one, a conforming one. Memes, although some can be resurrected such as Doge, are also revamped by new characters. The Chad vs Virgin was temporarily eclipsed by the hulking Doge and cowering Cheems memes.

The Simps:

THE SIMP IS a white knight who transcends political boundaries. The simp thirsts after pussy, behaving excessively cringeworthily to rush to the aid of a mildly distressed damsel, while forgoing any semblance of a bro code to massage his insecurities with momentary attention from a 5/10 female. A simp, more often than not, is a low testosterone male who cannot obtain a stable relationship with a woman who respects him because his attitudes are thoroughly undeserving of respect. White knighting of all definitions is cringe to outsiders, but a simp goes to extraordinary lengths and even loses friends and clout to simp to girls whose takes, positions, or easy virtue are provably unpopular among men with marginally higher levels of self-respect. Here is the operative word behind simpery: self-respect. Neither does the simp, nor does the woman simped to, boast any abundance of self-respect. Both are symbiotic. They feed off each others' validation, plastering over the void where their self-respect should lie. The simp, however, isn't necessarily a male feminist, but every male feminist is a simp. Male feminists often treat us to regular simp outs, demonstrating their poverty in conveying a non-threatening sexual energy when conversing to other women. It should come to no surprise that male feminists constantly find themselves on the wrong side of sexual harassment accusations; they cannot acquire a female partner via traditional courtship, normally due to some physical deficiency, personality disorder, or lack of non-lipid bodily development.

Simping simply reinforces many self-destructive behaviors of postmodern woman; she debases herself by flaunting her vanishing looks to audiences of sexually disaffected low-T young men, she pursues ethnomasochistic egalitarian politics, she was effectively liberated from the clutches of healthy family life to become an inferior version of an inferior careerist man. Simps don't really care about the women victimized by their simpery. As long as they use their funds and social media accounts to get their dopamine rocks off to a surrogate form of e-prostitution on the part of the simped e-thot, the wellbeing of the woman in question is largely ignored. The structural and familial reasons behind the lack of virtuosity in many – but not all – e-girls' short lived careers is downplayed by the simp's insistence that the woman is empowered and in control. The simp is a perverse inversion of masculine initiative. Acting as a paypig to women they'd never seduce, they effectively take on a small role as provider of a woman they'd never meet, assuming the role of husband-at-large, without ever enjoying the other perquisites of being a husband.

As I previously outlined, there are simps across the political spectrum. Metapolitically, simps do not belong to one singular political ideology. However, simps are often excluded from their ingroup for their lack of loyalty for the group in order to continue their Don-Juan-esque delusions of grandeur. Countless men, who may have been stable providers and husbands to women in bygone eras, are now grovelling for the basest approval to damaged women. That's not to say that the simp isn't damaged.

In an age where masculinity is shat on from a great height, man – urban man, in particular – is faced with a bitter quandary. Either, overcome the artificially-imposed demasculinization by taking on responsibilities deemed outdated or unnecessarily by the cool bugman elite (gymgoing, rejection of materialism, deference to the transcendental, starting a family, owning property), or, go with the flow and accept the degradation of their masculinity, submit their masculine energy to guilt for their forbear's reluctance to simp; In other words, what has come to be known as the 'patriarchy'. Simping is also a form of reproductive strategy or sterility strategy. No self-respecting woman would take on a simp as a husband as he has failed to demonstrate marriageable qualities or prove his abilities as a stable provider – because he spends a significant portion of his disposable income on simping out.

The simp has become a popular archetype in social media circles. Simping isn't strictly limited to the political realm. Other communities such as gaming also have their simps. Simps also transcend race and socioeconomic status. Wherever one has the resources to simp, one may simp. One of the underlying reasons as to why simpery exists is because of the dissolution of the nuclear family. Women have been propagandized into believing an ephemeral career pandering to their vanity and insecurities is superior to a modest familial existence. Simps, more often than not, will have come from homes bereft of a strong father figure. The root of simpdom is single motherhood – a practice self-perpetuated by simpery.

Evolution of memes

MEMES HAVE EVOLVED in lockstep with political undercurrents. If we were to pick a year, any year, to begin noting the marked evolution of memes, we would have to turn to 2015. Trump's awesome rise to political prominence commanded significant energy levels – particularly from creative, young men who otherwise lacked purpose. And now, their purpose became engendered by Trump's ploy to gain political office. Running on high energy speeches and politically incorrect rhetoric which resonated with the abandoned, maligned, white working-to-middle classes, young artistically-gifted meme makers took to the internet. With their fingers on the pulse and their internet-savvy grasp on truth, memes took on a whole new politically apt dimension. Despite the prevalence of talented meme chefs, who would deploy their memes alongside trending hashtags or algorithms for their work – and message – to hitch a ride on social media trends, with coordinated assistance from message boards and servers, some wonderfully cooked memes would gain incredible popularity. However, amid the flight of stellar memecraft, came boomer-tier memes to pee on the parade. But Boomer memes didn't jostle Pepe-based memes out of the meme ecosystem. Memeing evolved in tandem with political events. When it started become clear that Trump went laxer on his main non-economic positions – immigration, the wall, etc – a large portion of his energetic base abandoned memesmithing Trump-related memes. Instead, they focused their energy on memes satirizing culture; in particular, a deepening metapolitical chasm between left and right. One specifically popular meme, the Nordic Gamer Meme – a statuesque cartoon of a manly blond steadfastly repeating "Yes" to quotes from an assigned 'brainlet' – often portrayed a stereotyped narrative being challenged, such as a feminist view on reproductive rights. The simplicity of the meme also polarizes internet culture and reveals a simplification in how information is consumed. There is almost an irreconcilable gap between how the left and right grasp the world around them, which can be viewed through the lense of memes. Something that has become a stagnant stereotype of the left has been their inability to meme succinctly; there's a certain roundaboutness to the argumentative messaging in their memes. But as I've previously established, left-wing memes are awesomely powerful in their real-life application. After all, they convinced entire generations of people to abandon traditional authentic values in favor of hedonism.

It would appear that memes retreated from the overtly political, not to the apolitical, but to the metapolitical, going beyond simple party politics. That's something which has been left to boomers. Doge, another highly popular meme, was commandeered by various groups to spread messages varying from politics, war crimes, and even foot fetishism. The cute Shiba Inu meme's greatest success when being recoded to spread political messages online was from the right. Whenever the left attempted to recode left-wing perspectives into Doge memes, it flopped horrendously. The left appears to have abandoned utilizing Doge to spread political memes on any major level. Additionally, memes, as I've already mentioned, have become increasingly simplified to reach a wider audience and to promote a tacit dialectical messaging of the traditional vs the progressive. In countless internet circles, the traditional has won out against the progressive – and continues to do so. But, given the release of several infographics, there's little interaction between both metapolitical factions. What appears to be clear is what could be reiterated as a metaphysical vs material battle assuming internet form. It has become evident that party politics hasn't brought much contentment. Memes, in essence, have become a parody of reality itself. But reality itself can be distilled into a leftist metapolitical narrative which conforms to the following truths: egalitarianism good, woman oppressed but good, whitey bad, orange man bad, masculinity bad, western society bad, borders bad, heteronormativity bad. This is a fairly grug-brained oversimplification of core tenets of the leftist epistemological lens. Everything that dwells outside the prevailing socially-accepted politics must be cast aside. However, some of these truths have taken on an apolitical stance. The average apolitical normie probably doesn't realize the underlying metapolitical connotations of the Nordic Gamer Meme, but understands, on some level, that when he owns a 'thot' who's pissed off by the Nordic Gamer's refusal to accept her easy virtue as a viable individual identity, that, in some way, the thot is in the wrong. He realises her promiscuous lifestyle is inauthentic, self-destructive, and symptomatic of a deeper issue probably stemming from daddy issues. But there's a metapolitical level to the disdainful thotish harpy: she represents a 'leftist' lifestyle; or, to be more precise, a materialist lifestyle – including the recent materialization of what conservatism represents. The fact that she engages in irresponsible acts of sexual congress without first pair bonding with her temporary paramours indicates a deep societal issue. But it's becoming denormalized and increasingly stigmatized – even among the average person who has exclusively imbibed leftist narratives throughout their life. Sometimes, there's a little instinctive tug telling the average person that what they've been spoonfed is wrong. Maybe 13 does do 50, maybe promiscuous women have deep-seated issues without exception, maybe there is more to life than just passing dopamine secretions, maybe men aren't all that bad, and maybe white people aren't merely incorrigible colonizers responsible for all the world's ills. In reality most internet memes are counter-memes. They counter the prevailing leftist meme which has become a surrogate for reality itself. To be red-pilled signifies to be awakened to the fact that what the media, academia, and entertainment industry propagates is simply an obfuscation of reality to misdirect and confound, thus cementing their position of power. Truth – or the concept of truth – and power have always been inseparable. They wash each others' hands. The truth itself has been violently abandoned, culminating in our present political arrangement where people with dissident views are e-terminated.

Since the young right memetic energy redirected their efforts away from Trump, there has been a rise in the so-called Groypers – a Pepe-esque toad, emerging as a meme. The Groyper, unlike Pepe the Frog, became embodied in a real-life decentralized grassroots movement in American politics to disrupt Conservative Inc events by asking unanswerable questions to expose their ideological clotheslessness. Pepe the Frog, conversely, became an international symbol of liberation following the Hong Kong protests, somewhat modeled on the idealized American concept of liberty. Interestingly, memes have begun to take human form, which, to some degree, underscores the importance of countermemes. As a result, powerful institutions are fearful of a rerun of 2016, which they would want to avoid like the plague. Their approach, lacking pragmatism, is partly their downfall, as it requires heavy doses of censorship – because labeling counternarratives 'fake news' failed. When countermemes are brutally censored, two things are exposed: first, the validity of the message of the meme; second, the desperation of those institutions to preserve any semblance of power. And, just a reminder, it has only ever been about power.

AFFLUENT LIBERAL WHITE WOMEN (AWFL or AWFUL)

EVERYONE HAS AT LEAST come across one liberal white woman. Turn on the TV and they're depicted in every other show. The affluent liberal white woman knows what's best for America, in spite of not knowing what's best for herself. Affluent Liberal White Women rarely remain within a stable marriage as they hurtle towards menopause. Their fiery personalities are often captured in memes – most notably the 'Karen' meme as an impatient, insatiable customer with a furious will to speak to middle management; or, as a callously cold divorcée who leaves her husband in the dumps, taking the children in the process. The Affluent Liberal White Woman proudly espouses liberal views uttered by their preferred talk show hosts and comedians. She also has a penchant for wine which her entire social media following might classify as borderline alcoholism. Her social media bios will be peppered with political buzzwords, hashtags such as #resist #nevertrump, and a blue wave symbolizing her optimistic support for the democratic party. Her social media activity will energetically mirror whichever contrived outrage the media disseminates, often expressing irrational fury for rival statesmen or child migrants, using the latter as emotional surrogates for the children they forwent or neglected in order to further their career. Much of the Affluent Liberal White Woman's worldview is constructed upon hard-left feminist theory exposed to them at college, evolving the mixed with Prevailing Socially-Accepted Politics from their affluent social bubble. A holier-than-thou haughty attitude accompanies them when intrepidly stating their socially acceptable views. They will sometimes apply their trendy vistas to everyday life according to every short-lived fad. By the time they've finished sermonizing the benefits of one trend, it has already become outdated. Crocodile tears will be shed to reinforce their discontent at the current situation while their discontent remains inauthentic, superficial, and a means to secure social status within their clique. Virtue signaling is of paramount importance – becoming, in itself, something of a vice. Politics is dictated by the most self-destructive, self-effacing, policies; often with the goal of a rewarding dopamine hit. The worst kinds of memes are circulated by this select demographic due to their tenuous grasp of non-affluent liberal reality. In spite of their meme-unworthiness, their personas are something of a memeish caricature. Rash and quick to pass judgement on those who wish to judge others, they can do no wrong. They rest with the highest self-assurance of the supremacy of their views – everybody else must conform to their worldview if they seek to project their progressiveness to others.

The moral crusade has become something of a raison d'etre for the affluent liberal white woman. Her sage moral superiority enlightens the most benighted middle American, releasing them from the confines of their narrow-minded bigotry and painful yearning for a time that resides in the past. She leads the way, embraced by dopamine-releasing fuzzy mantras. Some may accuse the affluent liberal white woman of sanctimony; lengthy opinion pieces, Twitter threads with an ethnomasochistic slant blaming white men for their current political troubles, their shrewd know-it-all-ness, but, most of all, the irrepressible superficiality of their character is what makes them into a unique minority. Jumping on board progress-related fads for social approval, rather than reinforcing their being, is a central hallmark to their character. They utilise politically-loaded buzzwords to step from one poorly-researched media-generated outrage to the next. Some decry their presence as 'white' feminism, which is garnering marked unpopularity among social justice circles – the affluent liberal white woman can denounce white people all she likes, but, sadly for her, woke women of color will never truly be her friend. And here we reach the crux of the affluent white female liberal: her overeducation. The AWFL lives in her own little bubble filled with insincere fellow acquaintances who are also overeducated. Her bubble is never exposed to countervailing viewpoints. She is drip-fed nothing but socially-approved progressive vistas hammered to death at her Ivy League college – anything else is problematic. Within these progressive vistas lies an anti-white imperative which focuses on denigrating white history causing much inner turmoil. It becomes a quest to simultaneously scold her ingroup while recouping social headpats from equally enlightened AWFL peers. Perhaps, in part, their inborn saviour complex crossed with a narcissistic self-debasement propped up by higher-than-average levels of intelligence and a fat alimony check creates the AWFL. One could imagine the fatherly scientist from the Powerpuff Girls tossing all of those aforementioned ingredients into a beaker to create the wonder that is the AWFL.

LITERAL BUGMEN

ONE OF THE bizarrest narrative promotions from the mainstream press has been entomophagy – the consumption of insects. Entomophagy has been spruced up as a nutritional alternative to meat for a world facing overpopulation and climate change. These inevitable future events can only be averted if Westerners can stomach a radical change in their diets, forgoing their favorite fleshy dishes for smaller critters. Interestingly enough, it only behooves a shrinking Western population to radically change their diets in order to avert an anthropogenic climate crisis or to mitigate the skyrocketing future demand for food to accommodate population explosions in Sub Saharan Africa and Southern Asia. Rather than tackle the latter crisis head on, Westerners are lulled into the idea of stomach-churning dietary habits to staunch their guilt. Narratives can be employed to normalize many taboo practices. Repeat something enough and it will become true, inscribed within public consciousness. Many narratives took years to become normalized. White guilt wasn't something accepted overnight; drag kids would've been rejected fifty years ago; some of the things taught in schools today would've been dismissed as communist propaganda not so long ago. The general shift of progress requires constant reiteration of narrative. Rather than allow for its tenets to reveal their veracity, the Narrative Complex – media, academia, entertainment – must constantly shoehorn narratives to fabricate a reality which conforms to the ontology of progress. Anything that dwells outside its orbit must be deemed 'hateful' and, therefore, be rejected – even if it is factually truthful.

The prospect of entomophagy hasn't enjoyed much success on social media. Users often express their discontent at this prospect. Just like the stellar unpopularity of 'drag kids', it hasn't deterred the ambitions of the mainstream media to attempt to normalize both practices. It was recently discovered that bots were created to masquerade as social media users in order to bring positive attention to entomophagy. Strangely enough, despite widespread potential consumer disgust towards a bug-based diet, the media continues to promote similar articles on a daily basis – dismantling any narrative concerning the media's status as market-facing, which would imply, competing, entities given the fact that they persistently write wildly unpopular articles. Another recent, and alarming, revelation has been articles depicting cannibalism as a misunderstood alternative. Strikingly, articles of this nature have spiked with no ostensible justification other than contrived sociopolitical reasons relating to globalist political interests. One would venture to question the intentions of those who indefatigably pen pieces urging the average person to adopt dietary habits which could alter their physique, depriving them of adequate nutrients. The Economist recently published a piece praising the benefits of meat and its growing availability among those in developing nations. So which is it? Is meat an irreplaceable staple or must its consumption be curtailed for the climate, or to feed billions of Africans who haven't been born? The media covers the spread: the multiple narratives it sows often contradict themselves in order to retain their monopoly on truth. For example, on the subject of immigration, we are often told by talking heads the wonders of diversity, yet, when this narrative crumbles, we are told that mass immigration is an inevitable consequence of colonialism and it is deserved – even if your country never partook in colonialism. Neat, huh?

Despite the relatively absurd nature of promoting regular articles calling for meat-replacement diets, pulling on the ol' heartstrings of those most invested in the anti-Western narrative, the bugman has similar characteristics to the AWFL – except her fading good looks. The bugman doesn't have classically handsome chiseled features. He is endowed with a more globular, wobblier profile. His weak mandible muscles drop whenever he's excited to consume product, only to get excited for the next product when the novelty wears off.

Big Bug

I WILL NOT EAT THE BUGS. I WILL NOT LIVE IN THE POD. I WILL NOT GET CHIPPED. Big Bug – the bizarre fanatical drive to push entomophagy on the masses is upon. Like with most narratives spun by The Narrative Complex, Big Bug is simply another inauthentic astroturfed push to normalize an otherwise undesirable practice within a Western context. Yes, several countries around the world consider bug-based dishes a delicacy – but the West rarely has found the need to do so. That is, however, until the revelation of urgent action needing to be taken by Westerners and only Westerners. While newly industrialized Third World countries such as China and India pollute on a massive unprecedented scale, Westerners – and only Westerners – are told to alter their lifestyles. These alterations are as extreme as anti-natalism to the tamer entomophagy. Concessions must be made for projected population explosions in the Third World, artificially fueled by Western charitable intervention. Westerners didn't just wake up one day and decide that, in order to save the environment, they must start washing down their McMaggot burger, Cricket McNuggerz, and cockroach milkshakes. No – this was completely inauthentic, contrived. Just like the wildly unpopular promotion of 'drag kids,' entomophagy hasn't been all that well received. In spite of social media bots launched to popularize bug food, their efforts have been in vain – so far. The idea is to find a replacement for farmed meat and a solution to feed the world. Of course, the anti-natalist efforts aren't pushed in countries undergoing population booms, which raises suspicions as to the intentions of those behind Big Bug.

Bugs, for Westerners, are only really a tasty meal alternative in times of crisis. Apart from a spiritual crisis of meaning, there is no current economic crisis at present. Therefore, there is no need to eat bugs. Climate alarmism with socialist solutions have been peddled for decades. Big Bug merely offers another solution to the alarmism. However, taking a step back and viewing the sudden promotion of entomophagy, humiliation seems to play a big role in Big Bug. It is humiliating and undignified to adopt a radical and unnecessary dietary change. Bugs, in Western consciousness, aren't typically viewed as flavorsome morsels – it is beneath the average person to do so. Humiliation destroys the spirit. Humiliation is often a desired side-effect to power dynamics: those who are in power have an easier time controlling a humiliated populace. A humiliated populace would be far less likely to rebel if they lacked the dignity to do so. With their backs hunched and heading looking down, their will-to-power is weakened. Those who aren't in power are likely to express resentment and undergo a downward spiral of self-deprecating behavior, favoring a consumerist society. The push to eat bugs is an assault on Western dignity, revealing contradictory narratives: 1) current human progress has never been rivaled 2) times are bad and you need to start eating bugs.

The purpose of this chapter isn't to kick off a debate on nutrition, but meat is a highly nutritious complete protein brimming with minerals and B vitamins. In men, meat plays a role in boosting natural testosterone levels and protein synthesis. While there are impressive vegan athletes, they very much are in the minority. Western sperm counts and testosterone levels are dropping, for a variety of reasons, and an elimination of meat from all diets would plunge T levels even more.

Perhaps a side effect of entomophagy is metapolitical: a lower T population is a less right wing population. A society with lower T levels are more egalitarian, less hierarchical, and more consumeristic. Higher T men, on the whole, have greater drive, ambition, and seek more meaning in life than mere economic productivity. Men with higher T levels seek to better themselves and are more resistant to accept humiliating social conditions. Big Bug serves to cheapen morale and increase the distance between the elites and the pod-dwelling rabble. Power – whose nature has become more complex following the introduction of technocapitalism, globalism, and narrative, in a multicultural, but secular society – will take an interesting turn in becoming more distinct. One cannot honestly imagine the elites to wholeheartedly adopt entomophagy. The difference in dietary habits will subtly delineate social class in terms of power.

YouTube

THE RISE OF YOUTUBERS floating counternarratives, raking in viewerships similar to the mainstream media has posed a threat to the prevailing socially-accepted political narratives, eliciting a Big-Tech-led backlash attempting to censor the flow of dissident opinions reaching wider audiences. YouTube itself played an integral part in furthering right-populist movements in 2015/6, as those alienated by the mainstream media found refuge in their favourite content creators on the platform who would try to decode and provide conflicting viewpoints to the default left-liberalism of the public consciousness. As a result, YouTube felt it necessary to fudge algorithms to save the liberal narrative by recommending establishment-approved content next to dissident YouTubers. Some YouTubers were altogether removed from the platform, under accusations of breaching the platform's terms of services. Tweaking algorithms to promote certain viewpoints, in itself, is a form of forging public consciousness and truth to benefit a certain elitist power structure founded on so-called liberal principles. Another example of how liberalism defends one of its contemporary tenets – egalitarianism – is by the asymmetrical use of so-called "Human Rights." The concept of Human Rights is often used to defend terrorists or those beyond realistic criminal reform, formed into a cudgel to attack Western and American interests. Fears of Human Rights abuses in third world countries has led to the failure to deport undesirable criminals. Western countries willingly exert their efforts into reintegrating hardened criminals into society, sometimes to devastating effect. Finally, the Narrative Complex, in all its nefariousness, has redrawn reality to serve its interests. Tampering with algorithms creates a certain inauthenticity with the views promoted. Instead of fully banning dissident views, they're buried under several layers of neoliberal propaganda. One incisive social media countermeme reads: "if there was no hope, their propaganda would be useless."

The Groyper Wars

THE GROYPER WARS were the first 'large' real-life butting of heads between gatekeeping establishment conservatism in the form of Turning Point USA and young dissident rightists. The events were marked by the so-called "Groypers" asking awkward questions in the Q&A section which cannot be answered by a right-leaning liberal worldview inherent in mainstream conservatism. Those who took issue at the Groypers' concerns were mostly establishment blue checkmarks who would pass off their questions as racist and their attitudes as childish. Many decentralized social media users in fact sided with the Groypers, whose cozy internet meme took on an anthropomorphic form. As mentioned in the previous chapter, this is, perhaps, the first time a metapolitical internet meme assumed a real-life form in America.

What the Groypers represent is a demand for a new right political force which rejects old Republican mantras huddled around supply side economics and the illusion of small government. It also rejects facile takes on political discourse and a mainstream McCarthyian fear of socialism. The mainstream right seeks to stop the wrong enemy. States are turning blue, not because the young have become more socialist, per se, but through mass immigration and demographic change. One of the Groypers' concerns is to ensure that America seeks to protect American interests, which, according to their gripes, does not.

While recounting the tale now makes one realize how quickly internet discourse runs, the example of the Groyper Wars underscores the state of hyperreality as real life has become suffused with internet memes. Many of the so-called Groypers never use their real names on the internet, but have taken their e-persona into real life.

CHAPTER
11

THE MARKETPLACE OF IDEAS

"Conservatives have spent too much time normalizing the Left as a legitimate sparring partner. They are crazed fanatics trying to crush us, they have been subverting our country for decades, and their mind poison should never have been mainstreamed in the first place."
—Patrick Howley, journalist.

"It is not the slumber of reason that engenders monsters, but vigilant and insomniac rationality."
—Gilles Deleuze

THE SO-CALLED "MARKETPLACE OF IDEAS" is something of a fraudulent concept packaged to middle-of-the-road centrists seeking to reach some form of meaningful discussion, with the brightest and best ideas winning out, leading to their real-world application via policy and change. However, this couldn't be further from the truth. The marketplace of ideas serves little more than a release valve to vent genuine concerns, only for them to fall on deaf ears of policymakers. Real people who impact real change will not be receptive to such a concept. If they were, they would fail to retain power for long, as stronger ideas than their very iterations as to why they are in power would surely jostle them from their position of power. Free speech is something of a social construct, an ideal. It's a meritable ideal and one to be striven toward, but, in reality, free speech is always a threat to the powers that be. This is why narratives that serve to protect the powers that be cannot survive in a marketplace of ideas. How would relegating man to the status of an interchangeable economic unit, flooding his neighborhood with third world immigration, deindustrializing his state in favor of cheap labor abroad, and furiously calling him 'racist' or depicting him as the world's highest evil ever stand up against counternarratives? Short answer; it can't. The marketplace of ideas is a fraudulent decoy, allowing those with gripes to yell into the abyss to skim off stress from his current condition. The marketplace of ideas is also rigged by algorithms and big money to promote liberal ideas over dissident illiberal ones. Big money is willing to throw a meatless bone to those starved for the truth. These small morcels usually come in the form of milquetoast liberal takes on populism or Islam, completely missing the point and the metaphysical reasons for why right-populism is on the rise and will continue to rise. Even the ineffectual milquetoast opinions spouted in the marketplace of ideas are never implemented. Like with mainstream conservatism, the liberal overtone of the marketplace of ideas acts as a rearguard defense in normalizing micro ideas while failing to do anything about the macro. The answer to the failures of liberalism is more liberalism.

Somebody once pointed out that the neoliberal establishment is apathetic to radical left-anarchists' destruction of property, as it is akin to throwing a tantrum-throwing child a coloring book to pacify them. Equally, the mirage of the "free marketplace of ideas" is synonymous to the before metaphor; but, this time, the tantrum-throwing child is the civilized centrist or classical liberal, genuinely interested in getting to the bottom of the truth. In realty, it is little more than a release valve for disaffected people, wanting to be in good stead with progressives despite their ideological disagreements. However, the sad thing is, these well-intentioned liberals will be tarred with the same "Nazi" brush as people further to the right. And while there may be hyper-nuanced fifty shades of socialist red to choose from, there's no nuance for rightists: they are all Nazis without exception. The left often makes similar claims that society has worsened in the past 50 or so years by their fallacious metrics or observations: society has become more racist, transphobic, xenophobic, sexist, etc, despite being fully dominant over Western culture, but they advocate for more power over culture in order to rectify their failings. Power is the only thing that matters. Hayek was right in his fatal conceit where he identified that academics and intellectuals overvalue their own intelligence; but another fatal conceit is to presume that 1) the continuation of civilization is a given and 2) people indiscriminately act in good faith when engaging in debate. The overarching belief in adversarial good faith has hypnotized many into thinking that their ideological opponents want the best for society at large. Rather, there is a widespread notion to deconstruct Western Civilization and use faux empathy to court power at the expense of more traditionally-minded groups. The other thing to consider is the likelihood of political figureheads – of either side – to exhibit traits of narcissistic personality disorder, sociopathy, or Dark Triad at a minimum. Anybody who has ever interacted with somebody of the above pathology will be well acquainted with their intransigence. Argumentation or statistics will not change their opinion – especially given the clout they enjoy.

Dictatorships such as China are not afforded freedom of speech to a large degree, but they never made any pretensions to preserve any form of liberalism. Also, the nature of power within a dictatorship, and how power is used is different. Here, in a two-party state, there must be some semblance of electoral process, some illusion of choice to the average person. However, the more it becomes apparent that big money sways which puppet politician gets to toy around with political office, the more calls for censorship arise. When public consciousness is geared more towards a collective recognition of their political structure resembling a dictatorship, censorship must, by necessity, increase to fully conceal where power lies. Ironically, by promoting censorship, it also reveals and confirms where power lies. Within a dictatorship, it is almost unquestionable as to who holds power. Within a political landscape which promotes the electoral process, power is thought to be held by the ruling party. When the illusion fades, censorship must increase to preserve power. Nobody would gentlemanly concede power without a fight in their rightful mind. The only reason why Westerners as a whole are afforded more freedom of speech than other countries – apart from cultural reasons – is because the democratic process, in the short term, obscures where power really lies. Free speech availability could be placed on a spectrum sliding on how 'democratic' a country appears to be vs how dictatorial. Free speech is a lovely idea, but it has been attenuated not only by governmental forces, but also by the self-policing concept of political correctness, which ties into the moralizing educated middle classes. It's not really held by politicians. Think about Trump's campaign promises; apart from bolstering the economy, has he actually managed to fully achieve policies which were demonized as being 'racist'? No, because they're illiberal, they can't be rationalized under a liberal worldview dominated by economics and statistics.

CHAPTER
12

METAPOLITICS AND POWER

"Where there is power, there is resistance."
—Michel Foucault

"I am not afraid of an army of lions led by a sheep; I am afraid of an army of sheep led by a lion."
—Alexander The Great

"This world is the will to power—and nothing besides! And you yourselves are also this will to power—and nothing besides!"
—Friedrich Nietzsche

POWER HAS EVOLVED significantly since the industrial revolution. Since being clearly demarcated in hierarchical fiefdoms, power slowly became more obscured and proxied. Who really holds power? It's harder to tell for the Average Joe. Some superficially cling onto the belief that the politicians they elect are the ones calling the shots – but who calls their shots for them? The system is perpetuated by a network of self-interest and interests. Political entities are like machines seeking connections, and, within the unbound nature of progress, where they will go, nobody knows. Ted Kazcynski called this network "The System," for Gilles Deleuze it was "Desiring-production" and "rhyzomes," Nietzsche called it "The Will to Power," Adam Smith called it "Self-interest," but the fact remains, however you look at it, power exists and will always exist wherever humanity ventures.

"The high time preferences exhibited by society is reflected in one-man-one-vote democratic party politics where politicians play off the proneness to present minded temptation of the electorate, promising them things now without drawing their attention or intellectually rationalizing the potentially negative future consequences. Politics is structured to cater short election cycles where fiscal and monetary policies can be weaponized to secure power. Instead of looking towards preserving stability or demographics, one-man-one-vote party politics with short election cycles can only operate in a society where the electorate is more present minded. It is a self-propagating system which is destined to collapse – either through economic or demographic chaos, as a result of unsustainable short term thinking. Now, everybody can play the role of God in reshaping society to their liking. Current politics offer a facade of choice. In reality, the only choice they have is to consume and vote for one of two viable candidates beholden to special interests, lobby groups, and their egos."

Foucault points out how power in some cases is overt and brutal. For example, he alludes to a particularly gory execution of a man who attempted to assassinate Louis XV in 'Discipline and Punish'.

Now, those outside of the liberal paradigm who promote dissident views are something of an outcast, as Georgio Agamben calls 'homo sacer' barely recognizable as a human being – almost a persona non grata on steroids. Dissident activists who speak out against the neoliberal order will have their bank accounts closed, their internet wallets shut down, be refused entry to other supposedly liberal nations, and denied service from major corporations, all for holding the incorrect views. However, these views can be considered an affront to the order du jour. This is why they are wholly unacceptable. The point of departure for the liberal worldview is based on falsehoods – equality, globalism, multiculturalism, rationalism, progressive teleology – therefore, in order to salvage the weltanschauung of liberalism, further lies compounding previous lies must be spun. Eventually, the liberal corpus will become thoroughly unrecognizable – a mockery of what it used to represent. It is, notwithstanding, the same liberal entity, but facing the test of time. As it is metaphysically ungrounded, its form is irretrievably altered. Since the liberal order is so overwhelmingly powerful, to be otherized could spell a form of social suicide. People contentedly follow absurdities propounded by liberalism to avoid social ostracism. As part of its clutch on power, liberalism forms a rigid friend/enemy distinction. Whoever dwells outside the liberal friend zone is an enemy due to the perjudicial counternarratives held by that individual. Liberalism promises an enlightened man who is closer to the truth thanks to liberalism and the interiorization of sciences and philosophy. In spite of this, the truth has never been so temporary, as it keeps changing to suit a new liberal narrative. Remember, less than a decade ago, our liberal superiors were keenly anti-gay marriage – pre-supposing gay marriage is wrong, false – only for gay marriage to be okay – pre-supposing gay marriage is right, true. Truth can turn on a sixpence to favor those in power, despite being further from truth itself.

"Information always changes. Nothing that we know is stable, there is no objective truth to the Narrative Complex. Like dandelion seeds carried in the wind, falling wherever we land, only to be uplifted by another bluster of social change. Everything the Narrative Complex does conveys information. The social dynamics of a Hollywood movie emits metanarratives: metanarratives representing how life is to be lived, power structures, hierarchies, and representations of social importance. The peer review process in some departments is seemingly a politicized – how can I put this politely? – circle jerk. The news is unabashedly politicized, on both sides of the aisle, to fit the prevailing socially-accepted political narrative. Western governments are colluding with social media sites to minimize the distribution of so-called fake news, which funnily enough, has seen officials from more than one country ensnared by their own tyrannical laws. Anything outside of the prevailing socially-accepted politics must be extinguished as it presents an existential threat to the integrity of the narrative. If the truth it itself were on its side, then no measures to clamp down on so-called fake news would be necessary since the truth would self-evidently reveal itself to readers. The truth in itself is the eternal thorn in the side of the establishment. Without alternative media sources, Trump and Brexit may not have happened. These political events should never have happened, which indicates that the Narrative Complex hasn't entirely monopolized the narrative. On an individual level, all three heads of the Narrative Complex cerberus collaborate to promote constantly shifting values and information in order to keep the prevailing socially-accepted politics adherent dependent on their word and in a state of present mindedness for social, political and economic profit maximization."

Thanks to the rise of technology and the internet, speech has both been at its freest and most restricted, simultaneously. One the one hand, free speech can reach an enormous global audience, but, on the other hand, calls to censor and regulate the internet, preventing wide-reaching flows of dissident information from spreading is of utmost importance to preserve the liberal order. The edifice of power is founded on lies. What keeps the powerful in power is the narrative: the reconstruction of truth to create a moral framework and epistemology centered on furthering the interests of well-monied groups. This, in turn, requires socially engineering the masses into becoming perfect producing-consumers. A form of left-wing capitalism is a match made in heaven for those wishing to fatten their profit margins. Promoting traditional values or patriotism which isn't besotted by instant gratification would be deleterious to a liberal order, even if it doesn't directly attack it. The point is, humanity is currently dwelling in the most ontologically inauthentic age; nowhere has a society's virtues been altered to shun eternal principles – faith, family, nation – in favor of militant self-deification masquerading as atheism, self-sterilization, and aggressive ethnomasochism. What these individuals create, when they've become 'coolified' by the Narrative Complex is a world where meaningless thrills occupy the dead air between birth and death in the lives of many. Another thing to consider is the narcissism of those who promote said narratives. One simply does not get them to reconsider their worldview on refutation alone. Many of them exhibit behaviors that suggest they suffer from narcissism—but yearn to be sociopaths.

The neoliberal order has done a stellar job in immoralizing its enemies, by crafting a clear cut distinction between who are its friends and who must be opposed. Fear must be instilled to silence dissent. For avowed adherents of the prevailing socially-accepted politics, fear lies in the possibility of ostracism and dehumanization for failing to go along with the narrative du jour. Dissidents are unpersoned, have their reputations destroyed, and bank accounts closed. It is better to be feared than loved. The current order is both feared and loved and the same time. Secularism has granted the current order the opportunity to arrogate to themselves a clerical, if not, godlike status, cults of personality, and undying fawning adoration from the moralizing affluent middle class masses. But it is also feared by the same people. What would happen if they conferred support for Matteo Salvini, for example? Politics has assumed a religious streak, promising dire consequences for heretics.

Here are a few distinctions which can be drawn between supporters of neoliberalism/globalism/liberalism and nationalism/transcendental:

left:
> good
> moral
> intelligent
> kind
> tolerant
> generous

right:
> evil
> immoral
> dumb
> unkind
> intolerant
> stingy

The body representing the mainstream left has recoded specific words and identifiers linked to politics to gain and secure power. The idea that outside of politics there is no external metapolitical influence is thoroughly and painfully absurd. This is one of the fatal conceits of liberalism, that the body politic isn't swayed by other factors outside of political discourse. While there is some evidence suggesting that political views are somewhat heritable, current American society is bombarded by narratives urging people to abandon their prior beliefs in favor of a form of left-liberalism – which is now the default position for most apolitical Millennials and Zoomers. Reality itself has become superficially altered to accommodate a transition of power from nations to multinationals. Given how, for this particular thought experiment, the right is so maligned by almost every influencing authority on truth – the Narrative Complex – then why would anybody want to embrace these positions? Moreover, given how elections are held every four years, does one whose power and wealth depend on who is in power, really want the instability of regular elections? One of the greatest issues with modern party politics is the perceived instability of electoral politics. What can be accomplished in the short-term? Only policies with long-lasting consequences are provably detrimental. The introduction of the welfarist Great Society was one of the concrete fatal blows to the longevity of the American nuclear family. The 1965 Immigration Act was one of the fatal blows to Americanism in general. These policies didn't metastasize overnight. Across several years, where they imperceptibly corrupted the fabric of much of what it meant to be American. A one-term – or even two-term – president will not be enough to unfuck the situation. Change would need to be systemic.

Another addition to what could be considered a metapolitical association is the environmental movement. Environmentalism, by all accounts, would be viewed as being a left-wing cause within the public consciousness. Environmentalism, up to a certain point, is a moral good. However, environmentalism, in its current form, has been co-opted to shoehorn left-wing social policies and economic policies ending up benefiting big business – just a coincidence, I'm sure. After the fall of the Berlin Wall, reds became watermelons: green on the outside, red on the inside. Does anybody believe, given how China and Russia, being industrialized under communism, who now rank among the worst offenders against the environment, have a modicum of respect for the environment? Now, leftism, in its liberal form, has taken on an inauthentic environmentalism, at the crux of which, most consequences of its policies have anti-white outcomes. It's the Western World which has to make the bulk of all concessions. Of course, the narratives surrounding each movement has to change at a moment's notice – and it's by design. If there's no eternal truth, one is eternally beholden on the purveyors of truth, that is, the Narrative Complex.

GOOD AND BAD ELITISM

"The specific political distinction ... is that between friend and enemy."
—Carl Schmitt

PART OF THE DEMOCRATIC PROCESS, apart from factionalizing a country, requires a deification of one's political stewards. Objectivity is somewhat thrown out the window. Some elites are better than others. Perhaps one of the most crucial distinctions to be made in the interrelation between how the left and right view each other is perfectly summarized by the late Roger Scruton: "Leftwing people find it very hard to get on with rightwing people, because they believe that they are evil. Whereas I have no problem getting on with leftwing people, because I simply believe that they are mistaken." On some level, there's a metaphysical rift between the two; many adherents of the left believe their rightist opponents to be purely evil, incurably so. Part of the liberal worldview is a partial belief in the reformation of man. A violent rapist can be cured with love, tolerance, education, and a brief stint in a prison cell, whereas somebody who voted for Trump and believes that people aren't all equal is simply beyond repair. People on the right are evil for the sake of evil. Since it cannot be rationalized according to their worldview, they're simply defective. The violent rapist, however, was abused by his stepfather, beaten up as a child, fell into a world of drugs and alcohol – he is simply misunderstood, bereft of the love he deserved. The person on the right stands in the shadow of reactionary political movements from the early 20th Century. He cannot be reformed. His kids have to be taken away for their own safety and reeducated. Evil exists in the world without a purpose or observable ontology – it's just evil for evil's sake. But this is a facile take on reality. Glibly dismissing your political adversaries as evil for the hell of it misapprehends reality. Politics is a struggle for power. Complex interrelations of money, narratives, agenda, individuals, entities, organizations, all vying for as much power as possible. One of the things that impacts many political leaders is the realization that they don't wield as much power as they'd like. Even they have to jump through hoops. Power is decentralized, on some level, as every agent within a chain of command needs motivating via discernable incentive structures.

One of the reasons why the new left has been so successful in the past 50-60 years has been, in part, their ability to immoralize anything considered 'rightist,' 'western,' 'reactionary,' 'outmoded,' etc. A white Christian straight male patriotic family man is the pinnacle of all evil as he contradicts every tenet of what is packaged as progress. They've done a fantastic job in othering and exteriorizing anything that doesn't fit their narrative. But many on the neoliberal left are seemingly incapable of understanding the phenomenon of right-wing populism, embodied by Trump, Farage, Salvini, Orban, the FPO, Sweden Democrats, etc. To them, these glitches in the Matrix are impossible aberrations. Maybe there's an element of disingenuousness in their incredulity; perhaps they cannot face the possibilities of their ideology being incorrect, as that would trigger an identity crisis. It's easier to continue clinging onto their fracturing beliefs than admit their foibles. The superficial belief of your enemies being evil for the sake of evil is effective in creating a cause to exclude them from ever reaching power – for example, endlessly comparing right-wing populists to Hitler; Hitler being the sum of all evils. But depicting your enemies as evil, beyond all reform, also denies you the opportunity to understand your enemies better. The mainstream left's inability to understand the right-wing populist phenomenon is one of the many reasons why Trump's in office and the new left is losing popularity across Europe. Ted Kaczynski pointed out two major psychological traits of the leftist: first, oversocialization; second, feelings of inferiority. Here, we will focus on the first point, oversocialization. In the Victorian era, there was a torrential moralizing current spearheaded by the middle classes. Now, we witness a similar phenomenon. Instead of a revival of puritanist thinking, the middle-class left is a puritanical moralizing force. In the west, at least, leftism is strongly associated with the educated middle classes – as they can afford the luxury of sermonizing the average joe from the comfort of their ivory tower without ever venturing into the real world. Middle class cohesion, in part, necessitates oversocialization underpinned by intense moralizing according to a stringent, but constantly shifting, progressive framework. Fear of ostracism, for championing dissident non-PC views, feeds into oversocialization as well as the possibility of an identity crisis. A belief in progress is the glue holding the multicultural middle class urban project together. When a bank's ability to honor its notes falters, the bank's clients would cash their notes for something which retains its intrinsic value, eliciting a bank run. Progress isn't backed by anything except a series of entities seeking power. When the illusion of progress is revealed, who knows what will happen.

Although, to some, the right-wing and left-wing elites may have a lot of overlap in their personal interests, only the left-wing elites are presented as benevolent, beneficent, stewards guiding us to a brighter future. Cults of personality have been constructed around Hillary Clinton and the Obamas. They can do no wrong, in spite of accusations of dodginess. That's not, to say, that the right doesn't have their cults of personality. It's human nature to somewhat idolize one's leaders. However, given the secular nature of progressivism, there's an element of aggressive religiosity when revering their ordained establishment leaders. They are to be exculpated for their indiscretions – *cough* Bill Clinton *cough* – while continuing to champion their cherished positions, such as women's equality. Whatever the Narrative Complex tells us about their dear leaders is taken as gospel, no matter how logically inconsistent or contradictory the prevailing narratives may be. The right-wing elites may vocally support most of what progressives support, but it will never be good enough. In fact, as I've previously illustrated, many conservative economic policies have done more to further progressive causes than progressivism ever did, but still, it's a thankless job to try to get headpats from those on the other side of the aisle if you're viewed as a corrupt demon. George W. Bush can be friendly with Michelle Obama, but that tarnishes the angelic purity of Mrs Barry O. A Republican statesman can do more to further progressive ends yet be excoriated, vilified, and despised for the sin of being a Republican. Sometimes the sins of suspected rightism can't be expiated by a mere repudiation of one's prior positions – except if you're a neocon. Neocons who retracted their support for the Republican party when Trump won the nomination were quietly assimilated into the elitist East Coast fold. Resident NYT/WaPo-tier "conservatives" were gladly accepted to publish uninspired drivel attacking Republicanism – almost as if their allegiance lay somewhere else.

CHAPTER
14

THE BOOGEYMEN

"Whoever fights monsters should see to it that in the process he does not become a monster. And if you gaze long enough into an abyss, the abyss will gaze back into you."
—Friedrich Nietzsche

"What was right and true yesterday is wrong and false today. What was immoral and shameful— promiscuity, abortion, euthanasia, suicide—has become progressive and praiseworthy. Nietzsche called it the transvaluation of all values; the old virtues become sins, and the old sins become virtues."
—Pat Buchanan

"In all matters of opinion, our adversaries are insane."
—Oscar Wilde

WHO IS THE BOOGEYMAN of today's world? Aside from Boomers, which I have identified as having a white overtone, it's the nebulously defined amorphous mass of white people or whiteness. Constant Narrative

Complex invectives are launched at whiteness, condemning it as the reason for structural inequality and racism in largely non-white urban centers. It is not only allowable – but almost encouraged – to be anti-white by the stooge-like stewards of the Narrative Complex. As I have already mentioned, the fringe left is thoroughly anti-white in nature, but liberals, left and right, also lie on a spectrum of anti-whiteness. The liberals on the left welcome a Brazilified America with deep favelification of major urban areas. Of course, they would secure an eternally faithful voting base and the increase in population can be used to manipulate economic metrics such as the GDP, given the rise in potential consumers. The liberals on the right are unintentionally anti-white by failing to call out the elephant in the room – demographics – while prostrating themselves to liberals on the left to prove their anti-racism. Moreover, the liberal mainstream right's marriage to free market economics has been nothing short of disastrous in demographic terms. Unfortunately, an ideal of an unhampered market economy has been nothing short of a siren's song. In reality, the social changes ignited by the mirage 'free market' economics have brought about the unprecedented destruction of the family unit. Mass immigration from the third world was made possible from the liberal right's devotion to the so-called 'free market.' Metrics can be distorted by immigration, presenting an erroneous image of prosperity. Economic success has become the yardstick for human happiness. Economics, however, can be quantified. How can a society that lives for consumption be shown to suffer if the economy is booming – and if the economy becomes the pinnacle of human achievement? The evaporating white demographic can only be brought to the public's attention if it is presented positively. Several articles by neoliberal publications argue for lax immigration policies or outright open borders, as global economic productivity would surge. The vanishing white population is a good thing for X, Y, and Z reason couched in a myriad of progressive buzzwords. Only a hopeless romantic could decry the freight train of progress coming to enlighten you. But if any alarmist were to draw attention to the collapse in the white birthrate, they would often face dogpiling on social media by blue checkmarks and anti-white leftists – but I repeat myself. Before Trump's election, there was a massive upswing in overtly anti-white articles pumped out by the mainstream media. Trump's election slowed down the pace at which overtly anti-white articles were published. Despite the rise and fall of these articles, it would be difficult to argue that their prevalence was organic. In a way, these articles attempted to condition public consciousness for a normalization of harsher anti-white rhetoric. The Entertainment Industry already shoehorns various anti-white themes into their productions. Academia is less subtle with their anti-whiteness. If we were to consider what appears to be an onslaught against a shrinking white population – who have been successfully boogeymanned into a global metapolitical enemy – on all fronts, a new dialectic can be drawn up: anti-white vs white or nationalist vs globalist.

The end of history isn't (strictly) upon us; liberal democracy isn't the final dialectical synthesis or ideal. No, far from it. Instead, what has happened is that materialism has run its course – it can no longer satisfy the human spirit; people need something greater than themselves. If we were to run a crash course on the Hegelian dialectic (thesis + antithesis = synthesis), we could gain a crass understanding of post-enlightenment Europe. To begin with, liberalism revealed itself as the first thesis; which was met by socialism, it's antithesis; and, after much bloodshed, we have arrived at neoliberalism as its synthesis. These three positions are all secular and materialist in nature. Neoliberalism is characterized by the sanctification of private property and economic freedom of liberalism, but tempered by the egalitarianism and generous welfare (note: this isn't the original socialist position. Classical socialists would view welfarism, at the hands of social democrats, to be a reformist cop out) of socialism. Both positions are unabashedly globalist, which led to the reactive radical right-wing movements of the 1920s and 1930s – the rest, as they say, is history. The funny thing is, despite living at the end of history, there's a pervasive obsession in using the current year as a weighty argument to promulgate a slew of desired policies. It's 2020 (or to use John Oliver time, Current Year + 5), therefore, we must enable X, Y, and Z. It is the battle cry of the high time preferences; the people whose very essence is unanchored, grounded in nothingness. Since we are at a certain tenuously measured point in time in human history, roughly four centuries after enlightenment, so, how come we don't have all these things that my preferred worldview cherishes?

Despite the whopping power of the neoliberal order – the final synthesis – a growing movement rejecting the anti-white policies has emerged. The political left's fatal error was to abandon the white working class. Prioritizing diversity over the concerns of their constituents dealt a coup de grace to the left. People want something more. Appeasement through generous welfare and channeling the working class' energy against major corporations, plus the consequences of deindustrialization, isn't enough to win elections. Besides, the white working class' loyalty to left wing parties is on the rocks. Offering welfare is nice and all, but what good is it when they represent anti-white policies, more genders than Pokemon, intersectionality, and mass immigration? More politically active individuals want to live somewhere which resembles the place where their parents grew up, over a grey neo-Babylonian concrete jungle. But, for their troubles, they're given an earful of scornful epithets. And thanks to their stubbornness, the blue checkmark types are deprived of their grey neo-Babylonian concrete jungle utopia. It's all thanks to their intractable pigheadedness that we can't be living in a better world. Those bigots. May they rot. May they be replaced. Although there is no great replacement – that's just a conspiracy theory.

You may have been living in the Midwest for seven generations, but if you supported Trump in 2016, the chances are, unbeknownst to you, you could be a Russian Bot. The Russian Bot was the famed boogeyman for the neoliberal Democrat voting base –

Bernie Bros were less disposed to throwing the term around – in the 2016 election. The boogeyman is an evergreen, necessary, political tool. After the War on Terror reached a nadir in popularity, a new boogeyman needed to be found. And what better than the insufferably right-of-center white population? The Obama Administration inherited and worsened an already-botched series of entanglements in the Middle East and North Africa, and nobody was going to fall for the terrorist panic which ushered in an era of government-led mass surveillance anymore. Now, the Muslim population was kind, friendly, tolerant – fit for the neoliberal schema. Besides, they're also religiously loyal left wing voters in Western countries – a win-win. It was the gung-ho mentality of buccaneering whites who voted for neoconservative Republicans to unnecessarily take action. Of course, the constant anti-terrorist propaganda had nothing to do with influencing public opinion at all.

Every political order needs a threat to justify the possibility for the expansion of power and to give those in charge and their followers a raison d'etre. The main corpus of the left resembles something akin to a metacult, but lacking a deity and a rapture. Threats or boogeymen do offer an enemy to be defeated, satisfying the human spirit for struggle. Funnily enough, in spite of the left's egalitarianism, there is a strong need for heroic accomplishment, demolishing the egalitarian metanarrative of the left. Acts of heroism are now reserved for destroying anything impeding a more equal society. Consider how all former American heroes immortalized by statues and busts must come down. Lincoln, Grant, Roosevelt, Lee, Davis, et al, are too problematic to keep up, as protected minority groups might be offended. Therefore, the rest of you have to suffer the erasure of your history so that the hypersensitive must feel included, right? Partly. Imagine the power those activists must feel coursing through their veins by securing the removal of American historical figures at the drop of a hat simply by shrieking and claiming offense. Victimhood is how weak underachievers obtain power and pity. Power and pity, intertwined, form a nasty combo, promising increasing and more irrational demands to flex their cultural ascendancy on the rest of society. The removal of historical statues also exposes another societal ill: they're reminders of great – greater – men than the abundant pacified emasculated desk jockeys. Men cannot be reminded of an idealized greatness other than unimportant material gains in the forming of consumerism. This is why the future is female. The average cosmopolitan man must surrender his masculinity, his essence, his being, for women to give them a shot at commanding political, financial, and social power. The end result? American society, in part, resembles a cross between a glorified HR department and a nursery creche. On the one hand, there must be an aggressive push for fictitious notions of equality, diversity, tolerance, inclusion, etc, couched in corny corporate mission statement phrasing; and, on the other hand, the hypersensitive feelings of protected groups must be endlessly considered like a love-bombing narcissistic mother covering for the ill-behavior of their spoilt problem child. Things such as any -ism obstructs such progress. The battle to cure white people of their bigotry, in the form of their tendency to economically outperform some demographic groups and vote for the wrong party, is now an adopted mission transcending the individual. It gives purpose. It may sound perverse, but, when egalitarianism and globalism become the highest values, those who stand in the way of these ideals must be laid waste. From a revised historical context, whites today must pay penance for the sins of their ancestors. Had colonialism and slavery not occurred, America's white population wouldn't enjoy such material wealth today – which is why there needs to be a massive transfer of wealth from whites to people of color. This is one political narrative: whitey did something bad, whitey bad, whitey give money to disaffected PoC. The critical nature of historical revisionism and the blatantly outright communist political solutions to these historical wrongs proves that they're not in good faith. Moreover, some of the most radical egalitarians become biological essentialists/determinists at the drop of a hat when the topic of reparations to minority groups from white rears its ugly head.

Following on from a transcendent ideal supported by the more dogmatic members of the left, the concept of intersectionality, which hierarchically rearranges society according to the construed systemic oppression of each group. For example, blacks were enslaved in America for nearly two-and-a-half centuries, therefore, they've endured considerable systemic oppression, granting them a higher status within their intersections. LGBT folk have endured millennia of mistreatment and are also granted high status. Women were historically refused status or power on account of their womanhood, which is why they were oppressed. Obese people were maligned, denied proper medical treatment, which is why fatness is considered to be worth some oppression points. And so on and so forth. So, if you're a straight white male, where do you lie according to your intersections? Right at the bottom of the list. The only way you can redeem yourself is by constant self-flagellation, transfers of resources over to LGBT PoC, and then dying quietly – an offer too good to refuse! Although the concept of intersectionality appears unappealing to many, it is impossible to deny its anti-whiteness. But, hierarchically rearranging society in such a manner is a form of creating order. By elevating those previously thrown to the societal wayside, what the powers-that-be can acquire is unswerving fealty. This concept is known as Bioleninism, where status, office, and power is conferred to society's undesirables following socially turbulent times. Whites have been identified as the enemy; straight white males, in particular. The further away you can be from fitting the criteria of straight, white, and male; the better you are. Whiteness needs to be recoded to signify 'bad' in the public's consciousness. Why would anybody choose to be white? Flyers that read 'It's OK to Be White' are automatically excoriated as 'neo-Nazi', 'white supremacist', 'racist' – all buzzwords whose meanings cause a rabid Pavlovian response in antiracists from around the world, leading people to ask the question: 'so, it's not OK to be white?'

And who, in the last generation, deserves their statue to be built? Somebody whose physical courage, fortitude, and overcoming of odds superseded the average person. Very few, to say the least. One of the conditions of our current era is an amalgamation of egalitarianism and hyperconsumerism, leaving little to no room for heroes. We may not need another hero, given our luxurious material conditions, but we're certainly holding out for a hero. Yet in spite of hyperconsumerism rendering the average joe comfortably numb with a wide array of products acting as palliatives, there still seems to be an indirect demand for heroic antics. Everybody loves an underdog. Today's underdog has to at least own a few intersections – gay, female, non-white, etc – in order to qualify. Even heroism has been inverted. In 2016, Hillary Clinton represented an underdog-like hero facing the Russophilic internet frog-inspired force of evil trolling. She was a woman – which is a very important point to note. Had a Joe Biden figure won the 2016 Democratic nomination, I could guarantee we would not have been treated to so much saline catharsis on the night of November 8 of that year. This time round, at the time of writing this, Elizbeth Warren is a more diverse Hillary Clinton-esque candidate with her tenuous claim to Native American DNA and perhaps less skeletons in her closet. Whatever happens, Democratic presidential candidates are progressive more diverse, more well-financed, more astroturfed, and more emboldened by a metaphysical quest to stamp out a greater evil: whiteness.

Heroes these days aren't realistic. As they're fewer and further between, there's less of a connection to the heroes carted out by Hollywood. In our technological age, coupled with reason, cultural myths lose their symbolism, air of mysticism, and are, somehow, replaced by stories delivered by a different medium instead of written or spoken word. The delivery of communication and language itself has evolved to adapt to a technological, global society. This means that the written word has become emojified and simplified. Given the disconnect much of the younger generations feel towards their past due to the dissolution of many families beginning in the 1960s, and an increasingly globalist society, heroism ceases to be tribal, but universal, Marvelized. And in order to become universal and Marvelized, it must transcend national and tribal lines. To do this, heroism must become hyperreal – for it to belong to everyone, it must belong to no one. Heroes take on the form of the superhuman – as depicted in Comic books. Otherwise, not everybody can relate. Even then, with superhuman heroes, there's a failure in some parts to relate to certain heroes; for example, the Mary Sue who can defeat trained male fighters in hand-to-hand combat without any prior fighting experience. The hyperreality of heroes also serves to drive a wedge between human potential and human ambition. Although pre-industrial heroes had their stories embellished, the fact remains that several historical figures were capable of achieving unthinkable ends in today's terms. The availability of technology, in part, has lowered the physical being of man into becoming less independent, less capable. There's a reason why the bugman/soyboy meme is so popular: it encapsulates a growing stereotype of coastal urban-dwelling Last Men whose lives, meaning, and essence are dictated by leaps in labor-saving technological products exterior to them. Technology controls their lives. They live to consume product. This is the ideal. It's trendy. It's progressive. And having said all this, what's presented as progress in a heroic context is the ability to inspire a will-to-mediocrity for the Average Joe. This is usually broached in a cheesy monologue during the film's denouement. You have to be a devout antiracist; refrain from asking tough questions; promote globalism; stand for open borders; be a steward for progress; self-sterilize for the environment; relegate yourself to the utterly humiliating station of being nothing more than a faceless economic unit. For the elites, technology serves to solidify their position of power and contribute toward personal leisure; and, for everybody else, technology acts as an escapist palliative to anaesthetize the current reality of a purposeless economy-based reality, while bolstering net productivity.

Following on from the hyperreality of contemporary heroism, is the outwardly diverse nature of heroes. There has been an explosion in specifically non-straight-white-male heroes. The Narrative Complex's anti-whiteness has blazed the trail for this demand for non-straight-white-male heroes. Nowadays, not only are heroes hyperreal, but villains also follow suit. It has become almost politically incorrect to fail to cast a non-straight-white-male as a villain. If a blockbuster movie were to feature non-straight-white-male as a villain, they'd face a bombardment of criticism, boycott threats, and hit-pieces by the usual anti-white suspects. Throughout recent history, villains have often represented a contemporary enemy; during the Cold War, movie villains were often Russians. During the War on Terror, they were often Arabs. Now, they're almost always a straight white male.

If one were to study crime statistics by demographic for a couple of minutes, one would realize that there's a major discrepancy between what the Narrative Complex issues as truth and the truth itself. Thanks to the mass availability of technology, one can consume the Narrative Complex's positions du jour at the touch of a button. In 2001 movie, Training Day, one of the most famous lines – apart from 'My *N-word*' – is "it's not what you know, it's what you can prove." This phrase is of fundamental importance to understanding the impact the Narrative Complex has had in altering reality itself. The fact remains, straight white males have been attacked from all angles by all those who shape what can be determined as truth. Straight white males have been besieged and vilified by the media, academia, and the Entertainment Industry for a long time. The need for heroism still exists. And these efforts have been focused on the white boogeyman. The hyperreal Hollywood bisexual heroine of color will symbolically defeat the aimlessly cruel straight white male villain before enouncing an uplifting speech elevated by corny music. Popular shows such as the FBI behavioral analysis thriller, Criminal Minds – which has been running for several seasons – almost always features a white villain as an unhinged serial nutcase. The message is clear: the straight white man is dangerous. What's needed to protect wider society from this scourge is a diverse team of empowered minorities. If these people are so clement enough to include a straight white male tag-along, he must be effeminate, progressive, repentant for his whiteness, grovelling, and have the T-levels of a 95-year-old Alzheimer patient. Another part of this message is the fact that this straight white male isn't sexually available. A man of this description wouldn't be the best candidate for the role of a father. Hunkish masculine protagonists on TV are increasingly diverse. This represents a tacit form of sterility or fatherly incompetence from the straight white male actor.

Some may say that this isn't important, it's irrelevant, outdated, so on and so forth. But the fact remains that even the most ardently race-blind individual will be able to relate in some way. Eventually, when pressed hard enough, cries to the tune of "you're white, you deserve it!"; "white people have had their time in the sun, time to make for somebody else"; "that's racist"; etc., all admit the existence of the phenomenon of the boogeymanned white person, but allow for a combination of their emotional anti-whiteness and devotion to the progressive metacult to cloud their judgement. The pre-eminent white villain will be symbolically destroyed by the diverse hero – a perfect representation of modern politics. Whiteness has been redefined to mean "bad." As diversity is our strength, diversity means "good." Here, is the construction of the overarching American political dialectic in accordance with the Narrative Complex's truth: beneficent diversity vs an immoral shrinking white hegemony.

The mainstream right also has its boogeymen. The boogeymen here are a throwback to the McCarthy era where communism was a threat to America. Sadly, communism, being born out of a reaction to liberalism, has married liberal economics, and is now a living reality. Socialism, or creeping socialism, is feared. Socialism as an end itself is feared. The means by which socialism in America is to be achieved is largely ignored by the majority of boomer-tier conservatives. They proudly support LEGAL immigration, while their government ostensibly does the bare minimum to control illegal immigration. California didn't go Blue within a decade because Californians decided to become ultra liberal for the hell of it. No, it turned Blue just like Colorado, Nevada, New Mexico, Virginia, and soon-to-be Texas because of mass immigration – nothing else. The entire country could turn blue and mainstream conservatives could point to how wonderfully the DOW is performing and how socialism must be repelled at all costs. In a warped way, socialism has been identified to include mass immigration, but mainstream conservatives will point to how Hispanics – the bulk of mass immigration into America – are "natural" conservatives, despite boasting the highest rates of teenage pregnancy and steadfastly voting for the Democratic party at almost

3-to-1. The mainstream conservative adherent has identified the wrong boogeyman. It isn't an abstraction of socialism taking root; it's too late for that, the federal government has swollen to seven times its size under FDR. The conservative gatekeepers who harp on about socialism prevent conservatives from achieving any real ends. Moreover, their social accomplishments are non-existent, in part, due to gatekeepers misdirecting the efforts of grassroots groups concerned about limited government and the Constitution. In a few years, these groups won't have the social conditions to conserve any semblance of a limited government or Constitution. In fact, the federal government began its cancerous growth in 1913 – 52 years before the 1965 Immigration Act! In order to preserve a multicultural society, some very unconservative, illiberal, or unlibertarian things have to take place. First, the state must increase its size and scope to mediate any extra conflict and crime originating from introducing divergent groups in the same living spaces. Second, while there's a welfare state, other groups will consume welfare at disproportionate rates; especially when there may be a language barrier to overcome. Third, while there's an electoral process, as we have seen in every migrant exclave in America, migrant groups will eventually put forward candidates from their in-groups to impose policies to benefit their group over others. Fourth, restrictions on freedom of speech must be implemented to ensure harmony. Fifth, schools and prisons must require additional staff to cope with surplus demand. Sixth, reality must be further altered by The Narrative Complex to create an illusion of harmony for the multicultural experiment to persist. Seventh, society must abandon pre-existing cultural norms, architecture, religion, traditions, and so on, to be more accommodating and welcoming to other groups. Eighth, society has to become purely materialistic, determined by monetary value as the new country's Esperanto to bridge all gaps between each group. Conservatives don't realize that they've been boogeymanned themselves. They played themselves. They are the pinnacle of all evil, but try to appease their detractors, attempt to form reasonable dialogues, all of which is one-way traffic.

The other right-wing boogeyman is Islam. Fanatical hatred against Islam has been launched by many on the right. Islam, rightfully, has been blamed as being the ideological fountainhead for many terrorist attacks against America and the West in general. Many of these attacks come as a reaction to American interventionism in the Islamic World. Right-wing energy volleyed at Islam has led to further entanglements in the Middle East and justifications for American involvement in a dust-ridden hornet's nest of problems, thus further delegitimizing patriotism as it is repackaged for futile warring ends, rather than the protection of a culture or way of life. By focusing attention on Islam, the left has managed to make it a moral sin to be 'Islamophobic', which means that being against Islam makes you even more evil. While Islam isn't compatible with the West, cavalierly leaping into more entanglements only seeks to depopularize rightism locally for being associated as bellicose Islamophobes. Perhaps the sun has set on America's calling to be the policeman of the world. The world will never be fully safe for democracy. More young American lives shouldn't be committed to introducing feminism and drag kids to Afghanistan. America's new Manifest Destiny shouldn't be to become a despised polyglot cultureless strip mall, cracking the whip at insuperable backwater theocracies to follow suit.

CHAPTER
15

POLITICAL IMPOTENCE AND ANARCHO-TYRANNY

"Much of modern liberalism consists of people trying to get revenge on the football players they felt inferior to in school."
—Steve Sailer

"Better to reign in Hell than serve in Heaven."
—John Milton, *'Paradise Lost'*

RECENT GLOBAL EVENTS have proven the impotence of the American and other Western governments. With the recent coronavirus pandemic, the logical step would be to ground flights and seal off the borders while implementing rigorous quarantine restrictions, had COVID-19 been as deadly as it was supposed to be. But, in spite of this, the American government was one of the last Western governments to act. Consequently, America was the hardest hit country in the world. People from all around the world were vying to re-enter America, and the multiple interest groups and corporations were reliant on keeping travel relatively unhampered. Activists decried any effort to restrict travel to certain areas racist. What this all boils down to is that necessary decisions are impossible to make if you stand for nothing. Half-hearted, lily-livered, pallid efforts to contain what was thought, at the time, to be a deadly illness goes to show the sheer ineptitude of the federal government. Further, the recent George Floyd riots and Black Lives Matter protests demonstrates just how very little can be done to quell violence if it is in line with the prevailing socially-accepted politics. By extension, the Capitol Hill Autonomous Zone that sprouted out of a microcosmic power vacuum, in the absence of police presence, in a small segment of Seattle, following the riots, also underscores how if something coincides with progressive politics, it must be accepted. Had this anarchist commune been formed out of white nationalists or even mainstream conservatives, you can better your bottom dollar they would have been Waco'd or Ruby Ridge'd within a day or two. The fact remains, left-anarchism is acceptable to the prevailing progressive liberal establishment due to its similar social positions. Anarchism in general does not pose a threat to the progressive liberal establishment, despite claiming to militate against this monolithic superstructure. Destroying a small business in a riot benefits major corporations; an extra competitor has been taken out of the market. Small businesses have been hit particularly hard by this year's events; the coronavirus killed off much demand, the riots added insult to injury. The vapid materialist ideals echoed by many radicals help reinforce a consumerist society. We've all seen memes mocking radical leftists for their conspicuous consumerism, tweeting from iPhones, drinking Starbucks soy pumpkin lattes, wearing designer brands while professing a desire to eat the rich. Streaming services will portray these people as righteous and cool in their shows. Everyone on social media will support the protests. Major corporations will transfer millions of dollars to groups supposedly championing the oppressed. It doesn't matter if a few stores get looted in the process; society's energy at large backs the movement, winning over public consciousness and issuing further support for socially conscious megacorporations. Further entrenched within the progressive liberal establishment is the mainstream media who was instrumental in perpetuating the recent riots. When the killing of Ahmaud Arbery did not elicit the backlash expected by the media – who dredged up a story almost three months old, then artificially promoting the hell out of it – the George Floyd in-custody killing came along and blew the Arbery citizen's arrest killing out of the water. After this, the media disingenuously ran with the killing of Rayshard Brooks – a drunk man who fell asleep at the wheel in a Wendy's drive-thru, resisted arrest, fought with two officers, punched one, stole a taser, ran off and pointed the taser at them before he was gunned down – and a whole load of other strategically promoted white-on-black crimes to further stoke racial divisions. The mainstream media, at large, was wholly supportive of breaking COVID-19 social distancing for protests to take place. Pundits u-turned on their pro-social-distancing narratives to get behind the Black Lives Matter movement. Once the protests died down, the media attempted to surreptitiously return to their social distancing narrative, emphasizing the importance of lowering the rate of infection.

Colin Kaepernick began the whole "taking a knee" to protest the fact that he had been dropped for being a mediocre footballer. Kaepernick's PR stunt to salvage his teetering career became an international symbol protesting America's historic wrongs. Taking the knee, in less than a few years, has been adopted by some law enforcement and progressives of all stripes, supposedly to support Black Lives Matter, despite its anti-American founding. Within a couple of years, Americans can accept a gesture which fundamentally rejects the country they love. Some do it for dopamine hits from social media clout, others to placate protesters. Either way, one's emotional attachment to progress, on the one hand, and fear of ostracism, on the other, has driven many to turn on their country within a remarkably short space of time. A leading talking point on social media has been the spiritual conquest of Americans and Westerners as a whole. The gesture itself is a repudiation of one's country which for many appears to no longer be a higher purpose; the higher purpose has been consumed and spat out by progress.

CHAPTER
16

DIAGNOSIS

*"When we win, do not forget that these people want
you broke, dead, your kids raped and brainwashed,
and they think it's funny."*
—Sam Hyde

PARDON MY ALARMISM; those who might not be fully
aware of the sheer extent of how far into the last days
of Rome the American experiment has drifted –
you're in for a shock. America's main ideological
metacultural problem lies deep: to its very
foundation. America is unique. It is a country
founded on ungrounded liberal beliefs rejecting
European traditions. Its founders are motley
renegades; its original settlers reprobates, heretics.
America isn't founded on a deeper belief rooted in a
distant cultural line. It was never a 'Melting Pot,' per
se. Although before 1965, it had primarily accepted
Europeans from a diverse range of ethnicities, there
hadn't been integration to such a macro scale.
Granted, as a territorial enclosure, America
interiorized a multitude of different groups; however,
these groups hadn't seamlessly melted into one
overarching monoculture. America is peppered with

several ethnic enclaves. Among the various waves of immigration during the second half of the 19th Century, Europeans of different nationalities would be concentrated in clusters around the country. While certain groups did intermingle, there were still notable localized splits throughout – buffered by thousands of miles of land between coasts.

Liberalism, if anything, is a rejection of the metaphysical, the transcendental. Liberalism and capitalism are indissolubly linked. Capitalism isn't just an economic system – but a social order. Capitalism is the voluntary exchange of private property. And capitalism, in its liberal form, is arguably the first dialectical thesis of enlightenment; socialism being the antithesis. Pursuit of the material must necessitate an abandonment of faith on a societal scale. The most economically advanced nations are also among the most atheistic. Material wealth, in some ways, acts to reduce stress induced by financial worries. Stress is linked to religious beliefs. Religion acts as a palliative cure for stress in many instances. Unlike formal religion, liberalism doesn't offer any value system except to place property – the material – above all else. Liberalism isn't backed by the divine, and the Dollar isn't backed by anything truly tangible, rendering both subject to infinite inflation and reiteration according to human caprice. It merely accepts all social permutations, no matter how unsavory, destructive, or undesirable, as initiating force against person or property would be a rejection of liberalism. Did I mention you must be tolerant? An oft-cited quote, "apathy and tolerance are the last virtues of a dying society" couldn't be truer. However, that society is already dead, not dying. Tolerance implies a fundamental collective lack of belief in that social body's founding values. Liberalism is merely a transitional phase between one value system and the next dominant will-to-power because it isn't grounded in the transcendental. A new transcendental belief system underpinning a stronger political belief system will inevitably replace the existing political structure. They, too, have conned themselves into believing the End of History fairytale. Of course, the state can place liberalism as the highest virtue to the point where it becomes a moral imperative to impart liberalism globally; manifesting today as Neoconservatism. Afghanistan must go from a strongly traditional – and unforgiving – unconquerable (except in the case of its conversation to Islam) theocracy to wholly accepting of free markets, feminism, and sexual liberation all within a few years. Europe took over 500 years to get from internecine religious wars to unbridled effete tolerance. The rest of the world simply isn't ready for such a drastic change. Too much faith has been banked on the blank slate theory – anything else would be racist. And, as we have plentifully established throughout the course of this book, racism is a secular mortal sin – quite literally. Outrage mobs will celebrate the death of somebody they deem to be racist; even if there's no evidence to back their claim. But this denial of reality IS guided by faith – faith in tolerance, acceptance, and open-mindedness. Unfortunately, many minds have been pried so open, their contents have fallen out all over the floor. Questioning liberalism from a Western perspective is a no-no. But if anybody from a non-occidental background wished to offer their critique, the liberal would welcome it with open arms in many cases. Why do you think many non-Western freedom fighters espouse some Marxian belief system? It is because it is opposed the liberal iteration of Western Imperialism. It also, somewhat, gives their cause further validity by rejecting liberal capitalism. Sometimes whimpering lip service is given in disagreement if their critique extends so far as to reveal the true nature of Western hedonism. Overall, we must interrogate what is tolerated vs what isn't: tolerance, it seems, only serves to accept beliefs, lifestyles, and individual acts which are a direct affront to white Christian Western values. Culture, language, narratives, and society at large has been hijacked to serve certain political ends which demonize white Christian Western values to no end. But it fits nicely into the liberal schema; the mainstream right, as I have previously illustrated, is tethered to liberalism and is, therefore, prevented from offering any viable solutions without destroying itself. The most fundamentally divisive part of liberalism's ontology is its implicit yet militant individualism. While its values lie in the material, individualism is its secondary quality. Its abandonment of the divine or transcendental, as the dominant value system, has signified the removal of wider unifying qualities. Many new arrivals to America don't see themselves as American. Many new arrivals aren't pressured into assimilating. Anybody who'd suggest to new arrivals to speak the language, adopt the culture, become American, etc, would be weeded out as 'racist.' In fact, new arrivals tend to turn with more enthusiasm towards their cultures and traditions due to their close proximity with other rival cultural groups. Lately, there hasn't been much assimilation. In the absence of a monopolistic culture, faith, or society, diverse and divergent groups compete within the social petri dish for impact, will-to-power, and ensuring resources to their ingroup. Despite the unparalleled leaps in material prosperity, liberalism, being ungrounded, has no fixed destination or wider purpose, but for the sake of liberalism. There will be no grandiose end of history, but the beginning of a less Eurocentric order – which will be interesting, to say the least.

Furthermore, incentive structures are arranged in such a way to reward socially undesirable behaviors. As I outlined in A Matter of Time below, there are no social pressures to act prudently or in a future-oriented manner. Incentive structures currently encourage negative behaviors at the expense of the spendthrift, productive, adroit. America's incentive structure are, frankly, a race to the bottom for all those whose priorities don't extend beyond themselves.

"Naturally, individuals respond to incentive structures and seek status, as being social animals. If one is socially rewarded for certain behaviors, they will act accordingly. The desire to free oneself from oneself, due to an odium for the deficiencies of one's self-image through propagandizing and perverse incentive structures, creates a will for inauthenticity propped up by the prevailing

narratives, leading to an abject lack of self-respect or meaning. The meaninglessness of time is a by-product of the perceived meaningless of one's life, which many desperately attempt to plaster over with consumer goods and entertainment which belong to a certain brand, which offer a form of identification."

With the level of blatant corruption exhibited by politicians, political solutions are seemingly out of the question. Immigration levels indicate an inexorable leftward shift. Politicians were unable to court the white working class left-wing vote with more rehashed economic policies. Instead of offering decent solutions to newly emerging economic issues due to globalizing economic trends around the 1960s, politicians opted for siding with non-Americans. The right stood idly by prattling on about non-existent boogeymen which died with the Soviet Union. The nature of the threat to America has changed – and they're part of it. Socialism and communism aren't ever going to make a comeback – or at least as we've known it. Information has changed and become commodified. Everybody has access to social media at their fingertips and can afford the ample luxuries wrought by the latest industrial revolution. It's not as if the majority of individuals are living in inhumane, frigid, filthy St. Petersburg slums; or a feudal ancestor-worshipping pre-industrial China; or even a humble Eastern European semi-autarkic country house. Tyranny in America is already here and it transcends party politics. Trump didn't drain the swamp – it drained him. Tyranny comes at the individual level where the average person is enslaved to their passions enabled by the excesses of America's economic pre-eminence. The incentive structure discourages undertaking any personal hardship to bring about a greater social end. It simply ain't worth it. While some might argue that America is an idea, they are, in part, correct: the odds of another 1776 occurring to fight ostensibly foreign tyranny are highly unlikely – it simply isn't the same country. Now, there's constant pressure to infringe upon the meat and potatoes of American law: the first and second Amendments. Liberalism couldn't save them. Ultimately, liberalism is self-defeating as it cannot defend itself without contradicting its very being.

ABOUT THE AUTHOR

ORWELL GOODE (a pun for "all well and good") is a Youtuber, blogger, and an economics masters degree student. His main interests lie in documenting the decline of the Western world and identifying economic policies which may shape society for better or worse. He is the host of the "All Well and Good Show" and the co-host of news round-up "Waking Up The West" on YouTube.

Made in the USA
Coppell, TX
19 December 2020

45984507R00115